THE ULTIMATE ENCYCLOPEDIA

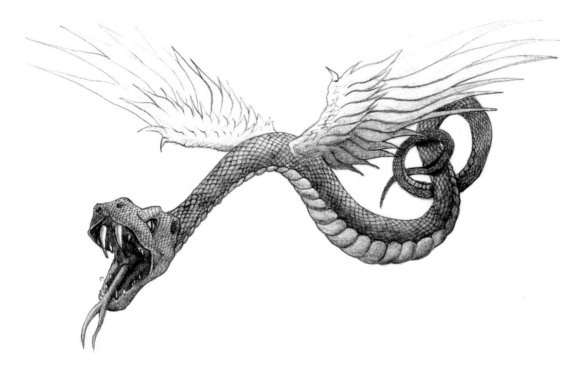

OF MYTHICAL CREATURES

DEMPSEY · COLLISON · ELVIN

BARNES & NOBLE
NEW YORK

Author: Colin Dempsey

Black & White Artwork: Paul Collison

Design and Layout: Emmett Elvin

Cover and Colour Section Artwork and Additional

Black and White Artwork: Emmett Elvin

Project Management: Kaspa Hazlewood

Production: Karen Lomax

2006 Barnes & Noble Publishing

ISBN-13: 978-0-7607-7460-1

ISBN-10: 0-7607-7460-9

Printed and bound in China

3   5   7   9   10   8   6   4   2

CONTENTS

FOREWORD

Whilst it may be tempting to think that the vast majority of the great mythical creatures are the product of our dim and distant past, browsing through this collection may give you pause to consider otherwise. Creatures that begin life as little more than urban legend can see their status quickly grow, often due to their ability to trigger something deep within us, something that fires our imaginations in new ways.

Many of the creatures in this volume have their origins in the 19th and 20th centuries. They may have sprung from fictional works reflecting the changing face of the world as with the Monster of Frankenstein or they may be based on eyewitness sightings, such as the peculiar cases of America's Mothman, or Central America's Chupacabra.

Humanity's interest with the powerful, the strange, the inexplicable remains undiminished across the centuries. Doubtless there will be gripping and entirely unpredictable new examples as this new century unfolds.

This book gathers all the greatest to date, from the earliest days of Athens through to the present day. Frightening or frivolous, powerful or pitiful, they are all to be found within these pages.

Emmett Elvin October 2005

INTRODUCTION

INTRODUCTION

Since the dawn of time mankind has been fascinated with the natural world. There were so many mysteries, so many unanswered questions.

Where does the sun go each night? Why is it able to reappear every morning? What happens to the heat of the sun in the winter months? How do we know for sure that it will return next year? What is this strange force which permeates the living world in spring, bringing forth green shoots from the earth and blossom from the bare branches? Why does the sea become so angry and then seem to fall back to sleep?

Nowadays of course we know the answers to these questions. But before the days of scientific enquiry we filled in the gaps in our knowledge with stories of nature spirits, tree nymphs and water sprites. We peopled the heavens with gods and goddesses who would hurl bolts of lightning at each other and make the sky quake with thunderous hammer blows. The earth was barren, and the trees bare because the Goddess of corn was in mourning for her daughter, kidnapped and taken down to Hades by the Lord of the Underworld. Mount Etna breathed fire and smoke because the terrible monster Typhon was

crushed beneath it when he dared to challenge the mighty Zeus.

Every star in the night sky has a story to explain its relation to the other stars and where it goes when it dips below the horizon.

Perhaps we have lost some of our sense of wonder at the natural world and that is why these myths and the fabulous creatures, which inhabit them, are now more popular than ever. Some have become so powerful as to enter the collective uncon-scious as archetypes. They tell us something about how we became who we are.

And then there are the creatures with which we love to scare each other silly.

We no longer have to hunt woolly mammoths, defend ourselves from grizzly bears, wild bulls and big cats. These animals would have been impressive enough to confront, but can you imagine the creature that you would conjure up if your father came home at the end of the day bloodied and bruised, trying to describe the ferocity of the beast he had to fend off armed only with arrows, spears and flaming torches. And what kind of form would you put to the snarling and growling you heard in the darkness outside the cave, beyond the flickering light of the fire?

Fabulous beasts, the kind that sometimes haunt our nightmares, belong to the deepest recesses of our minds. They are compelling, irresistible, absolutely riveting. Movie monsters such as Predator,

Alien, bogeymen like Freddie and Jason, speak to a part of us, that will never go away, no matter how rational or enlightened mankind becomes. The recent success of the Lord of the Rings trilogy,

describing a land populated almost exclusively by mythologi-cal beasts, speaks for itself.

I know that my adult mind has been shaped by these characters that I met in stories, read to me as a child. And yours probably has too.

As regards this present volume, the limits of space have made a few cuts necessary but I have tried to include all the old favorites as well as some new ones. If you are just dipping in for fun then I hope you enjoy it. If this is the starting point for more detailed research then I wish you good luck. It certainly is a most interesting and rewarding field of study.

Colin Dempsey.

CREATURES
A TO G

ABOMINABLE SNOWMAN

In Western literature prior to the twentieth century there is scarcely any reference to the Abominable Snowman or Yeti of the Himala-yas, although the folklore of that beautiful and haunting region is full of tales of a wild, ape-like creature that walks upright like a man but is covered in fur.

The first recorded sighting by a Westerner was in 1925 when N. Tombazi, the expedition photog-rapher of a geographical survey of the area, was awoken by his sherpas, and saw a strange figure that "showed up dark against the snow and as far as [he] could make out, wore no clothes. Within the next minute or so it had moved into some thick scrub and was lost to view."

Unfortunately Tombazi did not have time to take a photograph nor did he do so when he later examined the footprints left by the mysterious creature. He describes them as "similar in shape to those of a man, but only six to seven inches long by four inches wide at the broadest part of the foot." This is peculiar in itself because most accounts of the Yeti tell of a footprint much larger than that of a man's, whereas this is distinctly smaller.

He goes on to add, that "from inquiries I made a few days later I gathered that no man had gone in the direction of the footprints since the beginning of the year." The most convincing piece of evidence regarding the Yeti is a photograph of a footprint taken by Eric Shipton on the Menlugtse slopes in 1951. The footprint, shown by the side of an ice axe, is much larger than the one described by Tomazi and remains an enigma because it can neither be proven to be genuine nor fake. However its reputation has suffered somewhat by another photograph taken by Shipton of a trail of prints, which were always thought to be that of the Yeti, turning out to be the tracks of a mountain goat.

The only other "proof" of the existence of the Yeti, other than sightings and footprints, has been the yeti scalps owned and jealously guarded by several Tibetan monasteries. In 1960 Sir Edmund Hilary returned from an expedition into the Himalayas with one of these scalps and subsequent examination showed that it came from the pelt of a rare goat called the serow.

As for the footprints, it has been conjectured that a footprint of an animal or a man can freeze and then melt and then freeze again so that the original shape becomes distorted.

And Tombazi's fleeting glimpse? Well he himself has said that what he saw may well have been " a member of an isolated commu-

nity of pious Buddhist ascetics, who have renounced the world and sought their God in the utter desolation of some high place, as yet undesecrated by the world". And there are indeed monks, who through meditation and self-discipline, have trained themselves to survive temperatures no ordinary man could survive.

Perhaps the sightings are tricks played on the eyes in the blinding snows, perhaps the local legends have their roots in real encounters

with Gigantopithecus, an extinct ape bigger even than a full-grown Silverback.

After 1960 when the scalps were exposed as fakes, reports of the Yeti dried up and were replaced by sightings of his American cousin, Bigfoot.

And thus the Yeti seems to melt away under the hot light of Western scientific scrutiny but the legend refuses to go away.

ANGEL

Many cultures and religions have featured angels in their belief systems; the Assyrians, the Mesopotamians, the Hindus, Buddhists, Zoroastrians, Taoists, even the Vikings had their Valkyries who took up the souls of brave warriors who fell on the battlefield and brought them to

like spirits to search for the lost souls of ill or dying people.

There are many references to angels in the Bible and the Koran, usually in the form of heavenly messengers, intervening in the course of history at critical times. Amongst the most famous of all angels is Gabriel, whose influence on the biblical narrative is crucial. Not only does he appear to both Joseph and Mary, to reassure and to strengthen their resolve, but he undoubtedly saves the life of the unborn baby Jesus with his advice to flee to Bethlehem to escape the murderous Herod.

Angels, like mankind, exist and operate in a hierarchy. The highest are the archangels, of which there are seven : Gabriel, Michael, Raphael, Uriel, Zadkiel, Jophiel, and perhaps the most notorious angel, Satan himself.

The legend of the fallen angel provides a human dimension that was heretofore missing. This may be because there is almost no actual description of angels in the bible, and they seem to operate without any free will. Indeed, according to some Jewish scholars, a righteous man can rise above the level of an angel.

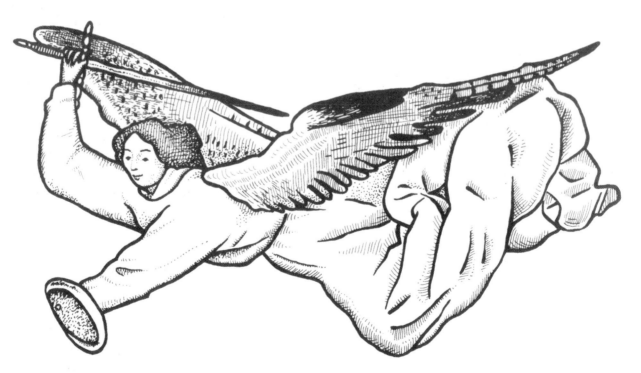

the halls of Valhalla. Devotees of Yoruba, a pantheistic African religion closely related to the cult of Voodoo speak of Orisha, spiritual beings similar in conception to Christian and Judaic angels and shamanic religions rely on bird-

Other significant angelic interventions are the occasion when Paul is freed from captivity, his chains loosed by a mysterious stranger, and the warning given to the three wise men to return to their homelands by a different route.

In particular Milton's epic poem, in which Lucifer is portrayed with more empathy than any of the hosts of heaven, contributes to this effect, and when he says "Better to reign in Hell than to serve in Heaven" it is a sentiment, with

which many of us can identify. Pride is after all an emotion that afflicts us all.

This dark side to angels, linked to mankind, has echoes in the story, barely touched upon in the bible, in which a level of angels known as the Watchers lust after the daughters of men and breed a race of giants.

Perhaps the most mysterious and unsettling angel of all is the angel of death that passed over the land of Egypt killing the first born sons of anyone who had not covered the lintel of their door in lamb's blood. Once again there is no description and we are just left with a sense of menace and dread. Other such instances of angelic appearance in a form other than humanoid is the pillar of fire and the tower of smoke set before the Israelites as they wander in search of the promised land.

Indeed it is quite probable that our modern western conception of the angel as a winged messenger owes more to images of ancient Greek and Roman deities such as Isis, Mercury and Nike than to anything in Scripture.

Below the archangels are many different ranks of angel, such as the Cherubim, the Sarim, the Irinim, and the Seraphim, also known as the fiery ones. Some of them are instantly recognizable, others described almost as though they are part of God's throne or chariot.

There have been many attempts to summon angels and manipulate them for personal gain, attempts which almost invariably have ended in deception and disaster, such as the research into black magic undertaken by John Dee.

In honor of his faithful service, Hera sews his many eyes into the tail of the peacock, her royal bird.

ARGUS

Argus was a monster famed for his watchfulness. His body was covered with eyes and when he slept they would close in sequence so he could never by caught off guard. Among the creatures who met their end at his hands were the fearsome monster Echidna, half woman half serpent, a bull that was marauding around Arcadia, leaving death and destruction in its wake and a cattle-rustling satyr.

His most famous exploit is the guardianship of Io, who had been turned into a cow by Hera to thwart Zeus's amorous inten- tions. Hermes was sent to whisk her away, but she was bound to an olive tree and Argus was ever watchful.

There are two versions of how Hermes accomplished his mission. In the first he hurls a huge stone at the monster, which dashes out his brains. In the second he dresses as a goatherd and the music of his panpipes is such a sweet lullaby that for the first time, all the eyes of Argus close at the same time. At that instant, Hermes draws his sword and cleaves the monster's head from his shoulders.

BANSHEE

The word banshee comes from both the Irish "bean sidhe", which means "woman of the fairies" and the Gaelic "ban sith", a spirit whose screeching and howling under the windowsills at night foretells the death of a member of the household.

Throughout time mankind has looked for omens that portended doom, both on a societal as well as a personal level. The Roman augurs were soothsayers who claimed to be able to predict the future by examining the entrails of sacrificial victims, studying the flight of birds, the timing and location of thunder storms and even the throw of dice.

In Celtic traditions, if a clock chimed at an inappropriate time or stopped, if a swarm of bees were seen at the door or if a rooster crowed at night it had an ominous significance. Death was not far

B

only ever warned families of pure Celtic blood and would not accompany them overseas if they had emigrated but could be heard in their home town if misfortune had befallen them on the other

BANSHEE CONTINUED

away and confirmation would be sought by keeping an eye out for anything unusual like a bird, especially the rook or raven, perched on a windowsill.

In Scotland, a "bean nighe", the ghost of a woman who had died in childbirth, could be seen, wailing and crying, washing the shrouds in the nearest loch, of those who were to die.

The banshee was thought to belong to the fairy world and dwell in fairy mounds, but to shun the society of other fairies. She was described as a smallish woman, wearing white, black, gray or brown, with long pale blond tresses and a waxy complexion. She would appear in the birthplace of the man or woman who was about to die, mostly in the early morning or late at night, and could be heard wailing from afar as she approached the house. Sometimes though not always she came right up to the windowpanes.

When she went away, there was often a fluttering sound as of a bird flapping its wings.

In Celtic folklore, the banshee

side of the world.
She also attached herself to places, such as crossroads, certain trees or streams, which then became imbued with an eerie atmosphere.

Many morality tales have sprung up around the myth of the banshee, especially regarding men who have offended her. Perhaps these old wives' tales were told to young boys to make them respect women, and live temperate lives. It is interesting to note that the banshee is always portrayed as a female spirit and it makes for a certain symmetry that mankind is brought forth into the world and ushered from it by women.

The Christian version of the banshee paints her as a demon, wailing for the souls that ascend to heaven and thus escape her master's clutches. She is also sometimes considered to be the soul of an unbaptized child or a woman who was too proud to surrender herself to God.

Another interesting theory is that the myth of the banshee evolved from the professional mourners who were paid to wail at the funerals of important people. They were often wizened old crones, dressed in black and paid in drink. Perhaps they found no respite in death, and were condemned to continue this office, as a punishment for their insincerity.

BASILISK

The basilisk was a creature as deadly as it was strange to behold. Pliny described it in his "Historia Naturalis" as "not more than 12 inches long, and adorned with a bright white marking on the head like as sort of diadem."

He also said that "it routs all snakes with its hiss, and does not move its body forward in manifold coils like the other snakes, rather advancing with its middle raised high. It withers bushes not only by its touch but also by its breath, scorches up grass and bursts rocks. It is believed that once one was killed with a spear by a man on horse-back, and the infection rising through the spear killed not only the man but the horse as well."

In fact so lethal was the breath, touch and indeed look of the basilisk that a warrior who had dipped his arrow in its blood, upon seeing the poison shooting up the shaft and into his hand, sliced it clean off before it could spread any further up his arm.

According to some, the only creature that could defeat the basilisk was the weasel. Pliny described how to "throw the basilisks into the weasels' holes, which are easily known by the foulness of the ground, and the weasels kill them by their stench

B

BASILISK
CONTINUED

and die themselves at the same time, and nature's battle is accomplished."

According to legend, the skin of the basilisk was often hung in temples to repel snakes and spiders and swallows and if the ashes of a dead basilisk were rubbed into silver, the silver could be passed off as gold.

In medieval times, as the myth of the basilisk evolved, it came to take on a new appearance, with only the lower half of its body being that of a snake, the upper half a rooster. Some artists also depicted the basilisk with wings, either covered in scales or feathers.

Several accounts survive of its birth. Alexander Neckam in his "De Naturis Rerum" tells of an egg forming in the body of a cock, then being laid in a dung heap and hatched by a toad. Other writers claimed that the cock had to be seven years old, that the hatching had to take place in the sign of the Dog Star Sirius and that the egg was spherical rather than oval and was covered in a thick membrane rather than a shell.

As its legend grew, rumor spread that there were other ways to kill the basilisk. The sound of a crowing cock was apparently lethal to it, as was the sight of its own reflection in a mirror, possibly because of its association with Medusa. The first basilisk was said to have sprung from her blood when she was beheaded by Perseus.

BEAST OF LE GAVAUDIN

In many rural areas it is still the custom, when summer arrives, to take sheep and cattle up to the high pastures that are inaccessible in winter. Often the children are sent to look after them. This was probably what the boy from the morality tale was doing when he cried wolf.

In the late seventeenth century in an isolated and remote part of southern France called Le Gavaudin, one such child, a young girl, was found with her heart torn out. Over the next few days more children went missing. Some were never found, others were discovered in a similar condition.

The remaining children were brought down from the mountains to the safety of the village and the peasants armed themselves and began to patrol the outer settlements.

A few weeks later, as the state of heightened tension began to die down, a woman who was regarded as rather eccentric, claimed that her dogs had been menaced by a rust-coloured creature, the size of a donkey, with short ears and a snout like that of a boar, which walked upright. Strangely enough it was the cattle that drove it away, because the dogs would not go near it.

It seems this was just the kind of thing the peasants needed to dissipate the atmosphere of fear they had been living under, for

the description prompted much merry-making.

But the next day, a peasant who was well respected in the village, returned from a hunting trip, with the story that he had surprised and shot at something in the woods, the like of which he had never seen before.

As news could only spread from mouth to mouth, some of the

more isolated farms had sent their children back up to the pastures in the belief that it was now safe to do so and there were more deaths. An appeal was made to the King of France, who sent soldiers to the region, after he was advised that the creature might be a loup-garou, a werewolf.

They arrived in the late winter of 1765 and actually managed to track down some form of beast and get a good shot at it, although it disappeared into the woods and no body was ever found.

As winter thawed, the children returned to the high pastures, and almost immediately another child disappeared. When his body was found, it was horribly mutilated. The soldiers came back and killed a huge wolf which had been terrorizing the flocks of a nearby community. Naturally enough it was assumed that the beast had been responsible for the child killings as well and so life returned to normal but this confidence was fatally premature.

More children were slain and soon entire villages were abandoned. Declining to wait for help from Paris, a huge hunt was organized, with every able-bodied man pledging not to lay down his arms until the carcass of the beast was strung up in the village square for all to see.

On June 19 in 1767, a full three years after the first deaths, beaters had flushed the beast out into a dense patch of woodland which could be surrounded.

It was spotted by a sure-shot named Jean Chastel, who had acquired some silver bullets, and he put two of them into its heart. Although the beast was paraded through all the surrounding villages, no reliable descriptions have survived and the location of its burial place is a mystery.

B

BEAST OF LE GAVAUDIN
CONTINUED

From what we can gather, it seems that the beast had small cat-like ears and feet that were a cross between hooves and paws.

It is most frustrating for cryptozoologists that the skeletal remains cannot be found, because this is one of the most detailed accounts of supposed werewolf activity on record.

Whatever the real cause of all those deaths-one huge and voracious wolf, several wolves, possibly rabid, or a homicidal maniac on the loose-there is the tantalizing possibility that it was the work of a loup-garou.

behemoth

Behemoth, much like Leviathan, is a monstrous creature, mentioned several times in the bible.

"Behold now behemoth, which I made with thee; he eateth grass as an ox. Lo now, his strength is in his loins, and his force is in the navel of his belly. He moveth his tail like a cedar: the sinews of his stones are wrapped together. His bones are as strong pieces of brass: his bones are like bars of iron. He is the chief of the ways of God: he that made him can make his sword to approach unto him. Surely the mountains bring him forth food, where all the beasts of the field play. He lieth under the shady trees, in the covert of the reed, and fens. The shady trees cover him with their shadow; the willows of the brook compass him about. Behold he drinketh up a river, and hasteth not. : he trusteth that he can draw up Jordan into his mouth. He taketh it with his eyes: his nose pierceth through snares."

As with Leviathan it is hard to tell what kind of creature, real or imaginary, is being described. Some scholars think that it is the hippopotamus, which can often be seen wallowing in the River Nile. The word could be derived from the Egyptian "p-ehe-mau", literally "water ox".

In Western minds they have a somewhat comic aspect, no doubt in part from seeing waltzing hippopotamuses wearing tutus in Disney's "Fantasia" and the graceful way in which they mince along the riverbed when their

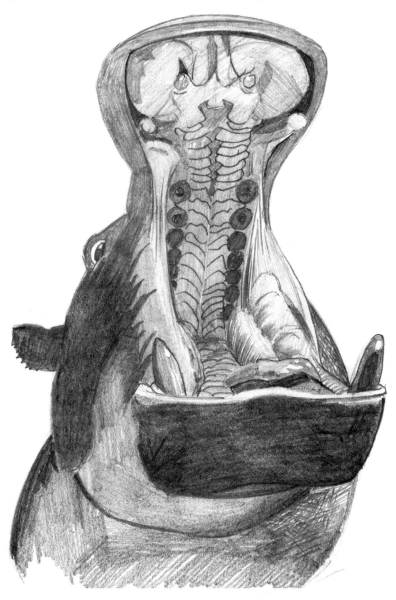

The sight of a fully grown bull hippo with its mighty jaws agape is an awesome sight. Could this be the inspiration for the behemoth myth?

weight is supported by the water. But they can be fearsome animals, especially when defending their young, and more people are killed by hippopotamuses in Africa each year, than by leopards and lions.

They can bite a man in half with the huge jagged tusks projecting from their mouths, and they will often capsize a boat if they think their territory is under threat. Ancient Egyptian gods that incorporated attributes of the hippopotamus and the crocodile were dark and malevolent and had to be appeased with offerings.

BEHEMOTH
CONTINUED

In the apocryphal Book of Enoch, both behemoth and leviathan are mentioned.

"And in that day will two monsters be separated, a female named leviathan to dwell in the abyss over the fountains of waters. But the male is called behemoth which occupies with his breasts an immeasurable desert called Dendain"

Elsewhere they are described as locked in mortal combat, the one with the other, sometimes at the beginning of time, sometimes at the end of days.

Nowadays the word has come to mean anything of monstrous size.

BIGFOOT

As long ago as 1884 there was a newspaper report in the Daily British Colonist, describing the capture in British Columbia of a creature "something of the gorilla type". The newspaper nicknamed the creature "Jacko" and modern-day opinion is divided as to whether this creature was an actual gorilla or whether the story is a hoax. It seems that hoaxing was pretty popular and the public enjoyed reading these jokes just as much as the journalists enjoyed writing them.

The name Sasquatch enters the collective consciousness in the thirties with the publication of a story written by J.W. Burns about a giant Indian Sasquatch who lived in the woods and had very long wild hair.

Local business leaders capital-ized on the popularity of the story by organizing Sasquatch hunts to bring tourists to the area and suddenly people started coming forward with accounts of their meetings with the wild man. Over time the wild man metamorphosed into an ape-like creature that walked upright like a man and the legend as we know it today was born.

William Roe's "first impression was of a huge man about six feet tall, almost three feet wide and probably weighing somewhere near three hundred pounds. It was covered from head to toe with dark brown silver-tipped hair, leaving bare only the parts of

the face around the mouth, nose and ears, making it resemble an animal as much as a human."

Albert Ostman went even further, claiming that in 1924 he himself was captured by a Sasquatch

family and taken back to their cave. At first he feared for his life but it soon became apparent that their diet consisted only of berries, nuts and roots. During the time he spent with them he was able to observe their behavior and

B

BIGFOOT
CONTINUED

reported that they communicated with a crude kind of language but did not know the secret of fire.

The presence of a hitherto unknown species of hominid residing in the desolate mountains of the Himalayas or the wilds of western Canada might seem plausible, but surely not in the relatively well-populated areas of Oregon and Washington? One would expect to find fossilized remains.

But there have been sightings south of the Canadian border of a similar creature, which gets its name from a photograph taken in 1958 by Jerry Crew, a bulldozer operator working in rugged terrain in northern California.

He made a plaster cast of a footprint he found outside his cabin one morning and posed with it for the newspapers. The print measured from his neck to his waist. Hence the name and it did not take long for Bigfoot fever to grip the nation.

As had happened with his Canadian cousin, the newspapers filled up with sightings of the mysterious creature although it is clear that they cannot all refer to the same animal.

One couple "driving along a remote mountain road east of the Cascade wilderness area say they saw a ten foot, white, hairy figure moving rapidly along the roadside."

Another saw "a beige creature, bigger than any human that walked with a lumbering gait." The most famous of all the Bigfoot sightings was by Roger Paterson and Bob Gimlin in 1967. The pair had gone in search of the creature in the wilds around Eureka in California and when they saw something moving in the woods up ahead they had a camera on hand. Astonishingly, the creature "covered in short, shiny black hair" was a female, "with big droopy breasts". The footage has been examined by scientists, and although some doubt has arisen regarding the long, loping stride which seems like a man trying to imitate a monster, they have been unable to prove it a fake. In the words of John Napier of the Smithsonian Institute, "I couldn't see the zipper and I still can't".

This footage prompted more serious expeditions, one of them sponsored by Texan oil million-aire Tom Slick, but once again nothing conclusive came up and Bigfoot remained as elusive as he or she had always been.

Much of the "evidence" is mere hearsay, some of it later proven to be groundless, such as the story told by a group of miners working in "ape canyon" near Mount Saint Helen. Apparently they were attacked by a bunch of apes standing seven feet tall, after one of the miners had shot at a creature he saw in the woods. All night long the apes attempted to enter their cabin, smashing rocks against the walls and when they had a chance to make a dash for it, they drove into town and returned with reinforcements but the apes had disappeared.

Much as one would like to believe this story, it turns out that many years later a man named Rant Mullens, who in his youth had worked in the area as a logger, said that one afternoon his friends and he had started rolling rocks down the valley at the cabin for a laugh.

One might have expected Albert Ostman to make a similar confession late in life, but he took the truth of the matter to his grave. So what are we left with? A photograph of a footprint that could easily have been faked. Film footage of what may be a man in a monkey suit. A legend that might have its roots in a sighting of a grizzly bear standing on its hind legs. Who knows? But perhaps the most tantalizing thing about the Bigfoot myth is that it seems to have followed in the footsteps of man's arrival in North America. There are tales of a creature similar to Bigfoot called the Alma in the wilderness of Soviet Russia. Then of course there is the Yeti in the Tibetan mountains, and the lesser known Chinese Wildman.

Did the creature cross over the land bridge that emerged in the Bering Straits in the Ice Age with the first settlers or was it just a myth that they brought with them to tell around their camp fires?

BLACK DOG

"I sprang to my feet, my inert hand grasping my pistol, my mind paralyzed by the dreadful shape which had sprung out upon us from the shadows of the fog. A hound it was, an enormous coal-black hound, but not such a hound as mortal eyes have ever seen. Fire burst from its open mouth, its eyes glowed with a smoldering glare, its muzzle and hackles and dewlap were outlined in flickering flame. Never in the delirious dream of a disordered brain could anything more savage, more appalling, more hellish be conceived than that dark form and savage face which broke upon us out of the wall of fog."

This is the moment when Sherlock Holmes and Doctor Watson finally come face to face with the Hound of the Baskervilles, the phantom beast that has haunted the family for generations.
Up until this point, the atmosphere of menace has been building steadily as we hear more and more about the legend of the hound. Watson and Holmes stumble across its huge paw prints left in the mud of the Grimpen Mire and hear its haunting spine-tingling howl in the dead of the night but we never get to see it until now. The genesis of the story, which

some critics rate as not just the best of the Sherlock Holmes series but the best classic English detective novel ever, is interesting in itself.

Sherlock Holmes had in fact been killed off by Arthur Conan Doyle, who thought that he was overshadowing his other more serious historical work. And so the last time we see him, he is locked in mortal combat with his nemesis Moriarty, the archfiend of crime. Watson watches in horror as they plunge to their supposed deaths

at the bottom of the Reichenbach Falls but significantly no body is ever found.

The novels first came out in serial form and when the last installment hit the shelves, traders in the city wore black bands round their arms in mourning, such was the affection felt for the fictional detective. Although he was determined never to write another Sherlock Holmes story, Conan Doyle eventually relented.

One day, during a golfing holiday with a friend in Cromer in Norfolk, the rain had kept them in the bar of the Royal Links Hotel all afternoon. The friend began to tell Conan Doyle about the local legend of a phantom dog known as Old Shuck, a huge black fire-breathing hound of hell with eyes that glittered with malice. He would appear at night on the outskirts of town, beside grave-yards and churches, haunting crossroads and desolate stretches of the coastline and anyone who saw him would be dead by sunrise.
Sometimes a lonely traveler wending his weary way home would suddenly become aware that a large dog was walking along beside him and then just as suddenly it would vanish.
The legend supposedly came to England with the Viking ships, the Norse word "scucca" meaning "devil".

Although the black dog would normally appear in isolated places, in 1577 in the middle of Sunday mass, the church doors at Blythburgh suddenly burst asunder and Old Shuck appeared growling and slavering. As he ran down the aisle and out through the back, the church tower collapsed and an old man and a boy died of fright. The scorch marks he left on the north door as he passed out, can still be seen to this day.

Old Shuck seems to be a regional variation of a phantom black dog that appears in local folklore up and down Great Britain. In Lancashire it is called Trash or

Striker, in Wales Gwllgi, the Dog of darkness, and in Yorkshire Bargest. In the Channel Islands the phantom dog is headless, supposedly the ghost of a man wrongly executed for murder.

Modern scholars believe that many of these myths were

work out the plot of the story that was forming in his mind.

The atmosphere of menace and supernatural dread of the bleak moors seemed a natural setting for his tale and as he drove around the countryside, his driver, who was called Baskervilles, told him of a

According to legend one of their ancestors had a faithful hound that followed his master around wherever he went.

After a long night of carousing, he was kept awake by his dog, which would not stop howling and

invented and perpetuated by smugglers or grave robbers anxious to keep people in doors at night.

The legend of Old Shuck really gripped Conan Doyle's imagination and he went to stay with a friend on the edge of Dartmoor to

noble family whose ancestral seat was in Claro Court on the Welsh borders.

The family had long been associated with a phantom hound and their coat-of-arms was a dog with a broken lance through its mouth and five drops of blood.

barking. Unbeknownst to him, the dog was trying to warn him of a wolf prowling around outside but the noise so infuriated him that he ran it through with a spear.
And ever afterwards whenever a Baskervilles died, a black dog would appear at night.

BROWNIE

The belief in brownies was especially prevalent in northern England and Scotland. Shy and secretive, it was almost impossible to catch a brownie unawares, but if you did manage to surprise him, you would see a shaggy little hobgoblin probably hard at work around the house, for there was nothing a brownie liked to do more than help humans with domestic chores like mending clothes and cleaning. Sometimes he could be heard at night, bustling away, and in the morning, everything would be spick and span, the hearth swept clean, the mantelpiece dusted, the boots polished.

If a doctor or midwife was urgently needed, he could summon them swifter than any horse and he even had the power to quell an angry swarm of bees and lead them back to their nest.

Every once in a while, a brownie could be taken with a fancy for mischief, and then he was a real pest, knocking over chairs, dropping crumbs everywhere, messing up the bed sheets, spilling the milk and spoiling the cheese. He might do this if he was offered anything other than bread or cream as a reward for his efforts.

In such a case, he could be got rid of by making him an outfit. When he tried it on, he would disappear.

CACUS

On his way back from stealing the cattle of the terrible monster Geryon, many strange and wonderful adventures befell the Greek hero Hercules. One night, as he lay sleeping near the seven hills where the city of Rome was later founded, a huge fire-breathing troll led some of the cattle back to his cave underneath mount Aventine. This Cacus, the son of the flame god Vulcan, was no ordinary imbecile of a troll. He was as cunning as he was evil, and he led the cattle backwards so that their tracks would appear to point away from his lair. He had also cleverly constructed a sliding door to conceal the entrance.

However, despite being well pleased with himself, he was not quite as smart as he believed, because he had separated a mother from her calf and when Hercules woke up, he heard the sound of lowing from inside the hillside, and so he started counted heads. On finding that he had been robbed, he flew into an almighty rage and immediately set about finding the culprit.

It did not take long to find the door to the cave, but when he tried to lift it up, Cacus, in fear

Above: statue of Hercules and the defeated Cacus by Bartolomeo Bandinelli, 1525-34

CACUS
CONTINUED

of his life, broke the mechanism that raised it. The door was hewn from such a large piece of rock that not even the prodigious strength of Hercules could budge it, try as he might, and this set Cacus to roar with laughter. The sound of the troll laughing only served to goad Hercules to ever greater fury and as he cast about for ways to force an entry, he spied a crack in the hillside. Setting his feet against one side and his back against the other he began to push and with one gargantuan effort the whole hillside came tumbling down. Agile as a cat, he sprang into the cave and flew at the troll, who breathed out a great plume of smoke to hide behind. But Hercules could see him by the fire under his nostrils, and he pinned him to the ground by his throat and choked the brute to death.

CALYDONIAN BOAR

Artemis sent a huge wild boar to the country of King Calydon, as punishment for his neglecting to honor her with sacrifice. There it wreaked havoc, trampling the crops and killing livestock and men.

According to Ovid, "his eyes glared with a bloody fire, his neck was stiff and hairy, his hide covered with bristles that stuck straight out like spears. He squealed harshly, hot foam streaming out over his broad shoulders, and his tusks were as long as an elephant's. Flames belched from his mouth, and the leaves were burnt up by his breath."

A veritable who's who of the classical world gathered to hunt the boar, the most notable of whom were Theseus, Jason and the heavenly twins, Castor and Polydeuces, the sons of Zeus and Leda, who was seduced by the god disguised as a swan.

Several of the hunting party met their maker on the point of its tusks. Ancaeus, for example, was gored in the groin as he was about to bring his axe down on its back. Atalanta was the first to wound it with an arrow from her bow and Meleager dealt the fatal blow. As he was in love with her, he presented the hide and head as a trophy, in honour of her deadly aim.

Pausanias claims to have seen the hide at Tegea, although the mighty bristles had long since fallen away and the tusks, three feet in length, were kept for a while in the temple of Athena in Arcadia before being removed to Rome by Augustus.

CECROPS

Cecrops was a man with the tail of a snake. It is thought that he sprang fully formed from the earth. Although actually the son-in-law of the first legendary king of Athens, the Athenians saw him as their founding father and he it was, who divided Attica into twelve communities and established many of the laws that ensured the civilization of society, such as ending human sacrifice and promoting the virtues of literacy. He was even said to have invented writing.

He was also the first to recognize Zeus as pre-eminent among the gods of Mount Olympus and from his time onwards, bloodless sacrifices were thought to be more pleasing to them. He introduced burials in the ground and oversaw the institution of monogamous marriage, providing the laws to ensure a harmonious and fair relationship. Modern scholars believe that his half human, half serpentine form symbolized his bringing together the previously irreconcilable natures of man and woman.

It was during his reign that the court of Areopagus was inaugurated, where the god Ares was put on trial for the murder of Halir-

rhothius, who had raped Ares' daughter.

He also arbitrated the contest between Athena and Poseidon, when they competed for the patronage of Athens, one offering a gift of the olive tree, the other a salty spring. The city was eventually given to Athena in gratitude for the wonders of olive oil. Poseidon showed his anger at

being rejected by covering Athens in a flood.

When Pausanias visited Athens in the second century AD, he claimed to have seen the olive tree planted by the goddess, and the cleft in the rock where Poseidon struck the ground and brought forth the sea-water. When the wind blew, he said, the sound of waves could be heard.

CENTAUR

Centaurs were very wild and dangerous creatures, only human from the waist up, with the body and legs of a horse. They were ruled by their passions, acting instinctively and violently. As such they represented the forces within man, which could be stirred up
and unleashed if care was not taken to subdue them with culture and civilization.

Above all, they should never be offered wine, and this was the cardinal error that led to one of the most famous incidents involving centaurs. At a feast to celebrate the marriage of Pirithous, the son of King Ixion, where the wine was flowing freely, all of a sudden, the centaurs who had been invited, tried to carry off the bride. An almighty battle ensued between the Lapithae and the centaurs, which was depicted on the south side of the Parthenon and can be seen in the British Museum.

The scene is one of extraordinary violence, the Lapithae hacking at the centaurs with their swords, the Centaurs striking back with their fists and hooves. In other works of art, they are shown fighting with branches torn from trees, or

drawing the chariots of Dionysus and Eros, the gods of revelry and sexual passion.

had buried in the ground, and as soon as he uncorked it, centaurs from all around, some several miles away, caught the aroma on the wind and attacked Hercules, who barely managed to drive them off with arrows dipped in the blood of the hydra.

with great honor, because he was one of the few wise centaurs. Chiron was another, skilled in the healing arts, who taught both Hercules and Jason. The son of Cronos and the sea nymph Philyra, he lived at the foot of Mount Helion. When he died, the gods set him among the stars, where you can still see him as the constellation, Sagittarius.

Hercules himself was killed by a centaur, Nessus, who had promised to bear his wife on his back over a raging torrent. Half way across, his bestial nature got the better of him, and he tried to drown her. At the sound of her cries, Hercules came running and he killed the centaur with a single arrow through the heart. As he lay dying, Nessus told her that should her husband's love ever dwindle, she should smear the centaur's blood onto his skin. He knew that the blood of the hydra, which was now mingled with his blood, would kill Hercules, and he would die in agony. Thus he had his revenge, for many of his brothers were shot down by Hercules when he visited the cave of Pholus.

When Hercules visited the centaur Pholus, he made a similar mistake, in demanding a draught of wine. Unwillingly Pholus unearthed a jug of wine that he

When Pholus examined one of the arrows he pricked his finger on the tip, and the poison killed him instantly. Hercules buried him

CERBERUS

Cerberus was the guard dog to end all guard dogs and the gates of Hades itself was his watch. He was a ferocious beast with three heads, three growling, snapping, salivating sets of jaws, and writhing snakes sprouting from his back. The poet Hesiod even asserted that he had as many as fifty heads!

His monstrous aspect was a product of the union between the giant Typhon and Echidna, a horrible beast, half woman half snake and he was the brother of two other dreadful ancient monsters, the Hydra and the Chimera. Such was his fearsome aspect that not a single spirit of the dead escaped while he was on duty but although he was able to keep watch in two different directions at once, some of the living did manage to get past him. Hercules managed to subdue him

CERBERUS
CONTINUED

with his great strength, although he was gored by his fangs, and even carried him off to the upper world to parade him around as proof of the accomplishment of one of his twelve labors. Orpheus, on his quest to find his dead wife Euridyce, lulled him to sleep with the sweet music of his lyre and

Aeneas and Psyche managed to soften his brute nature with some delicious honey cakes.

According to legend, when Medea tried to poison Theseus, so that her son would inherit the throne of Athens, she used the drool of Cerberus.

Cerberus by William Blake, from his series of depictions of Hell.

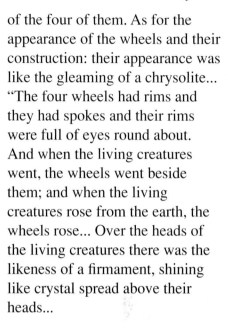

CHERUB

When we think of cherubim nowadays, we usually picture to ourselves the rosy-cheeked winged babies that adorn so many religious and allegorical paintings. But the cherubim described in the bible are altogether different more impressive beings.

The most famous encounter occurs in the Book of Ezekiel, where the prophet describes the spectacular arrival of four cherubim, carrying the throne of Jehovah.
"As I looked, behold, a stormy wind came out of the north, and a great cloud with brightness round about it, and fire flashing forth continually, and in the midst of the fire, as it were gleaming bronze. And from the midst of it came the likeness of four living creatures. And this was their appearance; they had the form of men, but each had four faces, and each had four wings. Their legs were straight and the soles of their feet were like the sole of a calf's foot; and they sparkled like burnished bronze. Under their wings on their four sides they had human hands. And the four had their faces and their wings thus: their wings touched one another, they went everyone straight forward, without turning as they went.
"As for the likeness of their faces, each had the face of a man in front; the four had the face of a lion on the right side, the four had the face of an ox on the left side, and the four had the face of an eagle at the back. Such were

their faces. And their wings were spread out above; each creature had two wings, each of which touched the wing of another, while two covered their bodies. And each went straight forward; wherever the spirit would go, they went, without turning as they went. In the midst of the living creatures there was something that looked like burning coals of fire, like torches moving to and fro among the living creatures; and the fire was bright, and out of the fire went lightening. Now as I looked at the living creatures, I saw a wheel upon the earth beside the living creatures, one for each

of the four of them. As for the appearance of the wheels and their construction: their appearance was like the gleaming of a chrysolite...
"The four wheels had rims and they had spokes and their rims were full of eyes round about. And when the living creatures went, the wheels went beside them; and when the living creatures rose from the earth, the wheels rose... Over the heads of the living creatures there was the likeness of a firmament, shining like crystal spread above their heads...

"And when they went, I heard

CHERUB
CONTINUED

the sound of their wings like the sound of many waters, like the thunder of the Almighty, a sound of tumult like the sound of a host; when they stood still, they let down their wings. And there came a voice from above the firmament over their heads; when they stood still, they let down their wings. "And above the firmament, over their heads there was the likeness of a throne, in appearance like sapphire; and seated above the likeness of a throne was a likeness as it were of a human form... and there was brightness round about him. Like the appearance of the bow that is in the cloud on the day of rain, so was the appearance of the brightness round about."

This vision has led some people to speculate that Ezekiel had an encounter with a UFO, that the wheels, the bright lights and thunderous noise are evidence of some kind of space ship.

When the chariot is later lifted up into sky, there is something eerily reminiscent of a spaceship about the description.

"When they went, they went in any of their four directions, without turning as they went, but in whatever direction the front wheel faced, the others followed without turning as they went. As for the wheels, they were called in my hearing the whirling wheels... And when the cherubim went, the wheels went beside them; and when the cherubim lifted up their wings to mount up from the earth, the wheels did not turn from beside them."

Earlier in the bible, the cherubim are equated with the winds upon which Jehovah flies: "And he rode upon a cherub and did fly; and he was seen upon the wings of the wind."

Such is their importance in the hierarchy of angels that they are sent to guard the Garden of Eden. "So he drove out man; and he placed at the east of the Garden of Eden cherubim, and a flaming sword which turned every way, to keep the way of the tree of life". And they even appear on the Ark of the Covenant, standing sentinel, wingtip to wingtip, and Jehovah is referred to as "God who dwells between the cherubim".

CHIMERA

The Chimera was a fire-breathing monster, with the head of a lion, the body of a goat and a dragon's tail. According to ancient Greek legend, she was the offspring of the monsters Typhon and Echidna, who also gave birth to the Theban Sphinx, Cerberus, the many-headed guardian of the gates of Hades, and the Hydra, slain by Hercules.

She was the scourge of the countryside around Caria and Lycia, terrorizing the people and devouring their livestock until she met her match in the Greek hero Bellerophon.

He had spent some time in Argos at the court of King Proetus, but when the King's wife fell in love with him he found himself in a tricky situation. If he rejected her, he would rouse her to anger, but if he returned her affections he would dishonor his host. He tried to prevaricate but the Queen saw through his ploy, and told her husband that he had tried to woo her. Unwilling to transgress the laws of hospitality by killing his guest, the King sent him to his

Chimerical creatures are part of the mythology of many countries of the world. This example is from Peru.

CHIMERA

CONTINUED

father-in-law with a letter asking him to do the deed for him.

And so Bellerophon was sent to

confront the Chimera in the belief that he would die in the attempt. Fortunately for Bellerophon, the winged horse Pegasus came to his aid and he slew the beast.

It is possible that this myth derives from a place high up in the forest of Lycia where natural gases beneath the ground send up flames though cracks in the earth.

CHUPAKABRA

The case of Chupakabra is a very strange one indeed. The trouble is that when describing it, nobody can compare it to any other known animal, and as a result it is very hard to imagine what it looks like. Pooling together witness statements, it would seem that it is about one and a half meters tall, and moves on its hind legs, which are thin and bird-like with webbed toes. It is difficult to tell what color its eyes are in the dark when it always seems to make its appearance, but they glow red when the creature is threatened.

Stranger still, it has a thin membrane that stretches from the wrists to the back like a bat, and its head resembles that of a kangaroo.

Another statement, this time from a zoologist, who claimed to have examined one, shot dead by a farmer, described its huge eye sockets, a knobbly spine like a crocodile's tail, and a hideous, mostly hairless hide with clumps of yellow fur bunched up in loose folds around the arms, suggesting the sails used by flying squirrels to leap from tree to tree.

Other eyewitnesses describe chupakabra as resembling a spotted, clawed alien type being.

Most sightings have occurred around farms with livestock in Central and Southern America with a few in Spain and Portugal. Before the first appearance, neighboring farms had been reporting that some of their sheep, goats and chickens were found in the mornings with small puncture marks on their necks and all the blood drained from their bodies. In fact Chupakabra means "he who drinks the blood of goats".

When the first witnesses came forward, their statements were so fantastical that they seemed to be the result of some kind of mass hypnotic experience.

One woman said she saw Chupakabra appear right out of thin air and then disappear again before her very eyes.

Miguel Agosto a garage owner claimed to have seen it hovering in the air, like a dragonfly and then vanish.

One chicken farmer, tired of its nightly depredations, set an ambush and managed to corner the beast. He struck at it with his machete and although he got a good clean shot at its head, the blade seemed to pass right through it as though it were a ghost.

Another witness describes blue marks left where she had seen Chupakabra standing.

Yet another claimed it had a dorsal fin which changed color when it took off, the fin seeming to hum and vibrate and when it flew away it did not flap its wings, rather it glided away.

So what is Chupakabra? Some kind of hitherto unknown large species of vampire bat? Mass delusion? A hoax?

One possibility is that it is an animal that has escaped from a laboratory experimenting with genetic manipulation on animal embryos. Another possibility, prompted by the fact that the folklore has followed linguistic and cultural traffic across the Atlantic from South America to Spain and Portugal, suggests that this is the Hispanic equivalent of crop circles, a hoax concocted and perpetuated by farmers in rural areas relying on their own imagination and mischief for entertainment.

CRETAN BULL

When the Cretan King Asterius died without a male heir, his adopted son Minos claimed to have the favor of the gods as his successor and furthermore he said he could prove this by asking Poseidon to send him a bull from the sea.

When the bull duly appeared, it was so beautiful that Minos reneged on his promise to sacrifice it, offering up one from his own herds in its place.

This dishonorable behaviour so angered Poseidon that he enflamed Minos' wife, Pasiphae, with a passion for the bull, which she was able to consummate with the help of Daedalus, who constructed a hollow imitation cow, inside which she was to wait. The child she bore was the minotaur.

For his seventh labor, Hercules was sent to bring back the bull from Crete and this was no mean feat as it was a magnificently strong creature, maddened by Poseidon who swore it would be nothing but trouble for Minos. In the end Hercules managed to gain mastery of the beast and he rode it over the sea to the palace of King Eurystheus, sitting on its back.

However, without someone of his prodigious strength to control the beast, it soon escaped and was marauding around the country-side, driving the inhabitants wild with fear.

CRETAN BULL
CONTINUED

King Minos' son Androgeous, a man of outstanding athletic prowess, tried and failed to capture it, meeting death on the end of its horns.

In the end, Theseus was able to subdue the beast and he drove it through the streets of Athens to the cheering of the crowds that lined the route and then he honored Apollo by sacrificing the bull in his name.

Theseus subduing the Cretan Bull, froma 5th Century BC vessel.

CYCLOPS

The cyclopes were a race of one-eyed giants, who dwelt on an island which ancient Greek scholars believe was modern-day Sicily. They were an uncouth breed of sheep- and goat-herders, with no concept of society nor of the laws or customs that civilized men live by. Making no attempt to build houses or roads, they sheltered in rough mountain caves with their livestock.

The poet Hesiod tells of three cyclopes Brontes, Steropes and Arges, the sons of Uranus and Ge, who made thunderbolts for Zeus. The most famous of all the Cyclopes is Polyphemus from Homer's "Odyssey".

He was a savage brute, renowned for his strength and cruelty, the son of Poseidon and the nymph, Thoosa.

Trying to find his way home to Ithaca after the Trojan War, Odysseus lands his ships on the shores of Sicily and sets out to find food for his men. Rather foolhardily he seeks out the company of Polyphemus to discover if the cyclopes really are as barbarous as their reputation suggests and immediately finds

himself trapped at the back of the monster's cave when he returns with his flock. The description of what happens next is very graphic indeed.

"He jumped up, and reaching out towards my men, seized a couple and dashed their heads against the floor as though they had been puppies. Their brains ran out on the ground and soaked the earth. Limb by limb he tore them to pieces to make his meal, which he devoured like a mountain lion, never pausing til entrails and flesh, marrow and bones, were all consumed, while we could do nothing but weep and lift our hands to Zeus in horror at the ghastly sight, paralysed by our sense of utter helplessness. When the Cyclops had filled his great belly with this meal of human flesh, which he washed down with unwatered milk, he stretched himself out for sleep among his flocks inside the cave. "

Not until four more of his men are killed does Odysseus get the opportunity to revenge himself and escape the monster's den. First of all he tells him that his name is Nobody and then offers some wine, which is greedily drained to the dregs. When the brute falls down drunk, Odysseus takes a sharpened stake and drives it into the monster's eye.

On hearing the screams of agony, other cyclopes from along the coast come running, however when asked who has done this, he replies "Nobody has hurt me!" and they laugh at him and leave. But now Odysseus has to get past the monster, groping about blindly at the entrance, gnashing his teeth. He tells each man to lash three sheep together and cling to the woolly underbellies and thus they manage to sneak out.

As Odysseus leaves the island he taunts the monster and reveals his true identity and Polyphe-

mus remembers a prophesy told to him by an old seer, Telemus son of Eurymus, that he would be blinded by a man bearing this name. In his misery at being outwitted, he hurls rocks at the departing ships and calls on his father Poseidon to rain misfortune on Odysseus's head, so that if he should finally make his way home, he will arrive alone and friendless to find trouble waiting in his own house. All of which of course comes true.

DRAGON

Dragon comes from the Greek word used to describe large snakes, "drakon", which in turn derives from "derkomai", meaning "sharp-sighted". It may be connected with the Greek and Roman conception of dragons as wise and all-knowing guardians not just of treasure, but of wisdom, which they might share with someone whose heroism and valor proved him worthy.

This sharp-sightedness was legendary, and it was almost impossible to outwit a dragon, but it might freely divulge its knowledge if you already possessed the insight to ask the right question, or even if it was impressed by the sheer audacity of whoever had come to seek an answer.

In this respect the ancient Greek and Roman dragon was more similar to the Oriental conception, than to the dragons of other parts of Europe, which where regarded as the incarnation of absolute evil. The association of the dragon, or great serpent, with evil, probably comes form the Near East, which

DRAGON

CONTINUED

has a large concentration of deadly venomous snakes that naturally found their way into the mythology of many of the cultures.

Examples include the Egyptian Apophis, the serpent of darkness, who was slain in battle each night by the sun god Ra as he passed

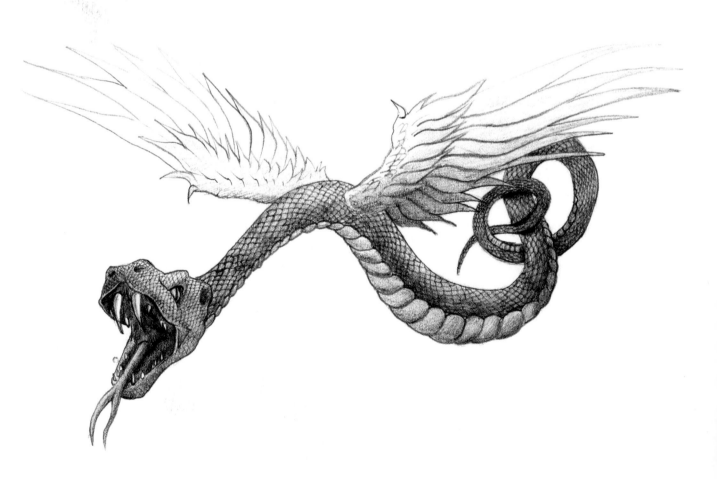

through his realm, and Tiamat, the mother of Chaos in the Chaldean pantheon, which looked more like the familiar dragon of today, with wings, legs and scales.

The dragon entered the Christian religion as the serpent of the Old Testament, associated with death and sin. By the time the Book of Revelations was written, this serpent that was once condemned to bite the heel of mankind, had become a monster of truly apocalyptic dimensions, synonymous with the Devil himself.

"And there appeared another wonder in heaven; and behold a great red dragon, having seven heads and ten horns, and seven crowns upon his heads. And his tail drew the third part of the stars of heaven, and did cast them to the earth: and the dragon stood before the woman which was ready to be delivered, for to devour her child as soon as it was born."

The pagan religions of Northern Europe were full of dragon myths, such as the great worm slain by Beowulf, but by the middle ages, Christianity has demonized paganism itself, and presents it as a dragon, slain by Christian knights such as St. George and St. Michael.

Dragons also feature heavily in the Arthurian legends. Uther Pendragon, Arthur's father sees a fiery dragon in the sky, which is said to foretell his ascension to the throne. Arthur himself dreams of

DRAGON

CONTINUED

a winged dragon and later meets one in battle, as do Tristram and Lancelot.

The pagan tales of treasure-hoarding dragons, dwelling under mountains and terrorizing neighboring communities, have filtered through to twentieth century literature. Many people's favorite example is Smaug, whom Bilbo Baggins encounters at the end of "The Hobbit". Like the dragon of the Middle Ages, he can fly and breathe fire, and his scales will turn any blade, although his soft underbelly can be pierced and proves eventually to be his undoing.

Perhaps the legend of the fire-breathing dragon grew from a Neolithic sense of wonder and fear at the awesome and devastating power of volcanoes. One theory supposes that the huge bones of massive extinct mammals, occasionally unearthed by ancient peoples, were assumed to come from some gigantic creature that lived in a subterranean cave. Another discredited theory holds that early man encountered some kind of dinosaur, but fossil records show

that there was an enormous time gap between the last dinosaur and the first men.

Such was its terrifying aspect, especially in Northern Europe, that many warriors decorated their shields and armour with images of the dragon, to strike fear into their enemies as they went into battle. The Vikings carved the prow of their ships into dragons' heads and later when Richard the First went

on his crusade to the Holy Land he rode behind a huge unfurled banner of a dragon.

On the whole, the dragons of the Orient have a friendlier more approachable nature and although they can be ferocious when roused to anger they will never devour a virgin. Indeed they are often actively sought out for their

DRAGON
CONTINUED

ability to dispense blessings.

There are two different versions of "lung", the Chinese dragon. The ordinary dragon has four claws, the imperial dragon has five. The Japanese dragon called "tatsu" has only three claws, and can change size and even disappear altogether. Neither dragon has wings,

although they are elementals of both air and water.

Various myths exist as to their genesis. One tells how the first dragon rose up from the deeps to the shallow waters and then set his sights on the heavens themselves. This angered the gods who cast him back down to earth to live amongst men.

DRYAD

A dryad or hamadryad is a tree-nymph whose spirit was thought to be bound up with the life of her tree. As the tree withered and died so her powers would gradually fade away. It was particularly dangerous to cut down a tree, without first asking permission, then making an offering and finally apologizing.

Nymphs were very beautiful and it was not uncommon for men to fall under their spell. They loved music and dancing and were sometimes consulted by mortals for their gift of prophecy.

The legendary successor to Romulus, King Numa was supposed to have married a tree-nymph, Egeria, and with her help his rule was long and peaceful. Her tree was an oak in a sacred grove by the Porta Capena, and at its roots there was a spring, where the Vestal Virgins would come to draw water. It was here that the King would meet his wife each night and listen to her wise counsel.

The nymphs of Greek and Roman myths are very similar to the Northern European concept of fairies.

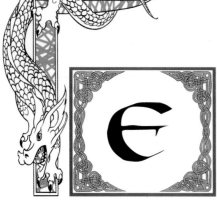

ECHIDNA

Echidna was an absolutely terrifying monster because she combined great beauty with repulsive bestiality. From the waist up she was a ravishing woman, below she was a speckled writhing python. She dwelt in a foul pit deep beneath the earth that reeked of rotting flesh, because of her habit of snatching anyone who passed the entrance to her lair and feeding off their raw remains.

The equally terrible Typhon was her mate and their vile progeny included Cerberus, Orthus the two headed guard dog of Geryon, the hydra, the sphinx, the Nemean lion, Phaea the great sow of Crommyon and the eagle that tormented Prometheus, picking at his liver.

She came to a sticky end herself when Argus the hundred-eyed monster caught her asleep and ripped her to pieces.

ELVES

Our modern concept of elves is of the kind that help Santa make his toys in Lapland or come out at night and mend the shoes of the weary cobbler.

They bear little resemblance to the elves, which originated in Norse mythology and came to these shores via Scandinavian folklore. The original elves were tall and powerful, beautiful and forbidding. Semi-divine beings, although not immortal, they lived long past the life-span of men. Old earthworks and pre-iron age hill forts were said to be the gateways to their subterranean realms.

Normally uninterested in the affairs of men, there was occasional interaction, even marriage and people of exceptional beauty, or gifted with talents, like musicians, poets or great warriors were said to be descended from such unions, in much the same way that Greek and Roman mythology makes men of prodigious strength the result of the seduction of a mortal by a god.

Nowadays "elf" has become synonymous with "fairy", "pixie" and "brownie". Shakespeare's "A Midsummer Night's Dream" is partly responsible for depicting them as tiny, winged, flower-dwelling creatures no bigger than an insect.
Thereafter it was thought that the circles formed by rings of mushrooms that spring up

ELVES
CONTINUED

overnight were made by elves dancing and it was dangerous to disturb these places.

The elves of English folklore were thought to be malicious pranksters, who tangled up girls' hair overnight making "elf-locks" and blew nightmares into the ears of sleeping children or made the skin prickle with nasty rashes. Sometimes they swapped a human baby for a changeling. Indeed to this day, the word for an imbecilic, misbegotten child, "oaf", comes from the Old Norse "alfyr" meaning "elf".

Flint arrowheads from the Stone Age were thought to be used by elves and found their way into witches' charms, as they were considered to be imbued with elf magic. This may have been an echo of the distant Norse belief that sacrificing to the elves could cure deep wounds received in battle.

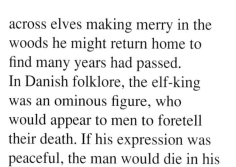

As with fairies, contact with the elves was dangerous. They were easily offended and capricious. A dance with an elvish woman, although a tempting prospect, could lead to a man dying from exhaustion and if he stumbled across elves making merry in the woods he might return home to find many years had passed. In Danish folklore, the elf-king was an ominous figure, who would appear to men to foretell their death. If his expression was peaceful, the man would die in his bed surrounded by loved ones. If his expression was one of suffering, then a violent nasty end was in store.

EMPUSA

Empusa was a daughter of Hecate, a goddess of the Underworld, worshipped by practitioners of the dark arts.

She was a nightmarish figure, with one leg of bronze, the other resembling the hind-leg of a donkey. She could also alter her appearance to make herself look beautiful and once a young man fell under her spell, she would drain his veins of blood.
She was not however altogether substantial and would disappear like a dream, if the young man only knew that to defeat her powers, all he had to do was to insult her.

In other versions of the myth, she was sent by Hecate to scare travellers, and if she caught them unawares she would eat them as they passed her lair.

As a shape-shifter she is similar to the Lilin, the daughters of Asmodai and Lilith who, according to early Jewish superstition, was the first wife of Adam. She was supposed to have turned her back on Jehovah, despite being warned that her children would become demons. They were wont to kidnap children and visit young men in the night disguised as beautiful women, enticing them against their will to have sex and then taking their semen, leaving them tired and irritable.

The lilin were thought to have engendered the medieval myth of the succubus, who tormented monks, tempting them to break their vows of chastity. The semen collected would be used by an incubus, a male demon, to impregnate a young woman in a grotesque parody of the Immaculate Conception and the child born would be an instrument of the Devil.

In many respects Empusa was very similar to Lamia, the queen of Libya who was envied by Hera because of the love Zeus bore her. In spite, Hera murdered her children and the grief transformed Lamia into a frightful monster.

Legend has it that she could not close her eyes and thus could not find respite from her unhappiness in sleep. So Zeus blessed her with the gift of being able to take out her eyes and thus find peace in oblivion.

Because of the memories of her own children she detested the bliss that other mothers enjoyed with theirs and would snatch them away to eat.

ERYMANThIAN BOAR

For his fourth labor, King Eurystheus set Hercules the task of capturing the Erymanthian boar, which had been wreaking havoc on the peoples and farmsteads of Psophis near its lair on Mount Erymanthius.

On his journey to the hunt, Hercules stopped by at his old friend Pholus' cave. Pholus was a centaur, but was kind enough to cook Hercules' some meat, even though centaurs always ate theirs raw.

Hercules' request for wine, however, troubled his friend, as Pholus knew the mere smell of the wine would attract his short-tempered centaur comrades.

Sure enough, shortly after Hercules took it upon himself to open the wine jar several centaurs appeared brandishing weapons and demanding to know who was drinking their wine.

A fight soon broke out with Hercules brandishing blazing sticks from the fire and pursuing the centaurs whilst firing his bow.

Back at the cave, Pholus pulled an arrow from the body of a fallen centaur. As he pondered how such

a small arrow could fell a full-grown centaur, the arrow slipped from his grasp. Its point fell onto his foot, killing him instantly.

Upon his return, Hercules discovered his accidentally slain friend and before returning to the boar hunt, gave his good friend a proper burial.

Guided by the sounds of loud rooting for food, Hercules soon found his porcine quarry. He taunted the beast from outside the cave where it dwelt, until it dashed out to confront its tormentor, snorting and bellowing. But it balked at the sight of the hero, an altogether different foe to the

lowly peasants it was used to, and it turned tail and fled up into the mountains.

Hercules was as swift and untiring as he was strong and he would not give up the chase. Finally it floundered in the deep snows of the high peaks and then collapsed from exhaustion.

Hercules Displaying the Erymanthian Boar to King Eurystheus From a Greek vessel with black figures, 5th century BC

FAERIES

The fairies with which we are most familiar are the dainty little creatures with wings that hover among the flowers at the bottom of our garden. Indeed when the two young girls faked the famous fairy photographs, which fooled even Sir Arthur Conan Doyle, they depicted the classic fairies from children's literature, the size and shape of Tinkerbell.

If you go further back in time, however, fairies are believed to be almost the same size as humans and in some cases even taller.

In "The Secret Commonwealth", written in 1691, Robert Kirk describes them as "of a middle nature betwixt man and angel". They were skilful magicians, and could change shape and disappear and transport themselves to distant locations at the click of their fingers. Relations with their human neighbors were often fraught, and they could use their magic to help or hinder, the decision either way often seeming absolutely arbitrary. One thing was for sure, once you had incurred their wrath, you were done for, and their revenge would be cruel.

There was much superstitious unwillingness to mention them by name for it was believed that this gave them power over whomever did so, and hence they were referred to as "the gentle people or "the good neighbors". For the same reason their color, green, was avoided, and travellers who had to pass through remote places, often left a part of their goods, whether this be tobacco or food, to appease them.

Sometimes they were appealed to for their healing powers, and they in turn might need the help of a human midwife. There are even tales told of marriages between mankind and the fairies, although, invariably they would not end well, as the fairies would miss their kin. Often these marriages would be based on some kind of deal, such as in the story of Wild Eric, who took a fairy wife, on the condition that he never mention

her background. When he could no longer resist, she returned to her kingdom.

Although the fairies seem to have been able to pass from their realm to ours and back again without consequence, the same could not be said of any mortal man who happened to stumble across theirs, which was often reached through a door in a hillside.

In spite of the warnings, if he was unable to resist the sound of sweet music, he would be lured away to his undoing. If he managed to return, earthly things would hold no pleasure for him, and he would soon wither and die or he might find that many years had passed in what seemed like a matter of minutes, and he would return to find his friends and family dead, and his name long forgotten. For this reason, it was inadvisable to fall asleep away from the village.

A gift from a fairy was a treasure indeed, and could bring great wealth, although rarely happiness. The fairy flag of Dunvegan was supposed to have been brought as part of a dowry, when Malcolm MacLeod of the Isle of Skye married a fairy queen. According to prophesy, the flag would save the clan from three great dangers, but only if it was unfurled in times of dire crisis. If it was waved for a trivial reason, three unfortunate events would follow: the heir to MacLeod would die, the Campbells would seize the group of rocks called The Three Maidens, and after a fox had given birth in a turret in the castle,

FAERIES
CONTINUED

the glory of the Macleods along with most of their lands would depart forever - there would not even be enough able-bodied men left to row a boat over Loch Dunvegan.

Needless to say, thanks to the foolish actions of one of the household, the flag was unfurled, and the prophecy fulfilled.

Another habit of the fairies was the theft of babies left unattended, often substituting their own children. Although they might look very similar, the mother could tell that something was wrong, and she had a changeling on her hands.

As regards the origins of the belief in fairies, one interesting theory proposes that the tales of the little folk could be rooted in real memories of an indigenous people

encountered by the Celts when they arrived in Britain. The Celts were a tall race, technologically advanced and territorially aggressive. They would have pushed any native tribes back into the interior, to live a secretive life, hunting and gathering in the thick forests. As in the fairy tales, there would have been occasional contact, kidnappings, the theft and spoilage of crops, perhaps even intermarriage. They may indeed have lived beneath the hills, in underground caves, and their knowledge of local medicinal herbs may over time have been transformed into magical powers.

Unfortunately, there is no archaeological evidence to back this theory up, and it is more likely that fairies are the watered down remnants of pagan gods and goddesses, both demonized and trivialized by the Christian missionaries in their attempts to convert the heathen races.

FAUN

The word fauns comes from the latin fauni, which were spirits of the countryside, much like the satyrs of Greek mythology, the attendants of Dionysus with goats' horns and legs. Later they were amalgamated into one rural deity inhabiting the pastures and fields, Faunus, who made the herds and flocks healthy, the soil rich and the crops ripe. He also loved to walk in the woods, accompanied by his followers. Everywhere they went, the birds sang and the leaves rustled in the wind, the boughs groaned under the weight of nuts and berries.

He would occasionally utter prophecies as in the Aeneid. When Aeneas arrives on the shores of Italy at the mouth of the river Tiber, he meets King Latinus, the son of Faunus, himself the son of Picus, who is in turn the son of Saturnus. Latinus seeks out his father to ask to whom he should give his daughter's hand in marriage.
"He sought a response from the forest, below Alburnea's spring, where Alburnea's wood, among all woods supreme, echoes to a lovely spring and breathes forth a malevolent sulphurous vapour. There does a priest first bring his offerings and then, lying on the skins of the sacrificed sheep spread on the ground, beneath the skies of the night invites a sleep. In it he sees many floating, monstrous images and hears voices of many a kind."

Faunus tells Latinus to give his daughter's hand to Aeneas and thus mingle his bloodline with a race of men who shall have the whole world at their feet, from the rising sun in the east to the setting sun in the west. These men are to be the Romans.

It is possible the association of Faunus with prophecy comes from the word Picus, which means woodpecker, as augurs looking for omens would often pay close attention to this bird.

Another name for Faunus was Incubus and in this guise he was associated with nightmares and buried treasure, similar to the Greek god Pan, who gave his name to the word panic, the sudden sense of claustrophobic fear when alone in the woods, especially near dark.

FRANKENSTEIN MONSTER

Strictly speaking, Frankenstein is actually the name of the scientist, not the creature whom he brings to life, which is unnamed, variously referred to throughout the book as the monster, creature or fiend. Its appearance is quite different to the heavy-browed monster with bolts though its head that we are familiar with from the celebrated performance of Boris Karloff.

"It was on a dreary night of November that I beheld the accomplishments of my toils. With an anxiety that almost amounted to agony, I collected the instruments of life around me, that I might infuse a spark of being into the lifeless thing that lay at my feet. It was already one in the morning; the rain pattered dismally against the panes, and my candle was nearly burnt out, when by the glimmer of the half-extinguished light, I saw the dull yellow eye of the creature open; it breathed hard, and a convulsive motion agitated its limbs.

How can I describe my emotions at this catastrophe, or how delineate the wretch whom with such infinite pains and care I had endeavored to form? His limbs were in proportion, and I had

selected his features as beautiful. Beautiful? Great God! His yellow skin scarcely covered the work of muscles and arteries beneath; his

Mary Shelley's original vision of the monster was one of male beauty horribly soured by reanimation.

with his watery eyes, that seemed almost of the same color as the dun-white sockets in which they were set, his shriveled complexion and straight black lips."

The idea for the story of Frankenstein came to Mary Shelley on a trip to Geneva, where she stayed in a cottage on the shores of Lake Leman. Nearby was Lord Byron, who had taken the Diodati Villa,

hair was of a lustrous black, and flowing; his teeth of pearly whiteness; but these luxuriances only formed a more horrid contrast

having left England for good.

Mary's husband Percy Shelley was a good friend of Byron and they spent a great deal of time together. Towards the end of summer, the rain kept them indoors and they entertained themselves by reading a recent translation of German ghost stories.

Late one night, Byron suddenly declared that they should each write a story. He began a tale of a vampire, which his physician, Doctor Polidori, was to finish and publish under Byron's name. Percy Shelley told a tale of his early childhood but Mary was at first unable to think of anything. "I thought and pondered vainly. I felt that blank incapability of invention, which is the greatest misery of authorship, when dull Nothing replies to our anxious invocations. "Have you thought of a story?" I was asked each morning, and each morning I was forced to reply with a mortifying negative."

However she was soon inspired by the exalted company she was keeping and the late night conversations which turned on the recent experiments of Doctor Erasmus Darwin and Luigi Galvani who had made a dead frog twitch by passing a current of electricity through its muscles.

After one such night she unable to sleep.

"When I placed my head on my pillow, I did not sleep, nor could I be said to think. My imagination, unbidden, possessed and guided me, gifting the successive images that arose in my mind with a vividness far beyond the usual bounds of reverie.

"I saw, with shut eyes, but acute mental vision, the pale student of unhallowed arts kneeling beside the thing he had put together. I saw the hideous phantasm of a man stretched out and then, on

The version of the monster portrayed by Boris Karloff in the 1931 Universal Pictures production has become the iconic image.

the working of some powerful engine, show signs, and stir with an uneasy, half-vital motion."

The story, which she went on to write, was well received by her companions but when a

novel-length version was later published, it created quite a stir. "A tissue of disgusting absurdities" was how one reviewer described it, "full of prose to make the flesh creep."

FURIES

Legend has it that the furies, or erinyes, sprang up from the spot where the blood of Uranus spilled onto the body of Gaia, the Mother Earth, when his genitals were severed by Cronus.

Uranus had fathered the Titans with Gaia but he was filled with hatred and fear towards them, so he forced them back into her womb. Armed with an adamantine sickle, Cronus lay in wait near the entrance and when Uranus tried to make love to Gaia, he attacked. Three drops of blood produced three furies, Alecto, Megaera and Tisiphone and they were charged

Orestes pursued by the Furies. From a painting by William Bouguereau, 1862

with preserving order and justice, punishing the most heinous crimes and administering vengeance on murderers whose victims cannot avenge themselves.

No mortal could stand the sight of them, so horrific was their appearance. They went on all fours, growling and slavering, sniffing the ground like bloodhounds to track their prey, their bodies crawling with snakes. Sometimes they are shown as winged, driving their enemies with whips, to demonstrate the impossibility of escape. In fact so relentless was their vengeful wrath that not even death could offer release from persecution as they often followed their prey into Hades to see justice carried out.

Both Orestes and Alcmaeon were pursued by the furies for the crime of matricide. Oedipus felt the sting of their whips after the fulfilment of his curse, whereby he killed his father and married his mother. Phoenix was punished for taking his father's lover for himself and their vengeance ensured he would die childless.

GARGOYLE

Literally speaking, the gargoyle is not a mythological creature at all but we thought we would include it to clear the matter up.

It is actually an architectural term derived from the French "gargouiller", an onomatopoeic word meaning "to gurgle" and it serves a functional purpose, taking water off the roof and away from the foundations of the building, hence the projecting form.

In classical times these water-spouts were usually adorned with the faces of lions and could be seen above temples such as the Parthenon and other large buildings.

In the Middle Ages the grotesque figures with which we are now familiar became popular. Perhaps this coincided with the vogue for decorating the outside of churches with evil spirits and demons to show that they could not enter the house of God.

The famous "gargoyles" on the parapets of Notre Dame in Paris are not actually gargoyles as they serve only a decorative purpose. They are chimeres.

GERYON

For his tenth labor, the cruel and callous king Erystheus sent Hercules to capture the cattle of Geryon. A lesser man would have drawn the line at this for Geryon was said to be stronger than the strongest man in the world, an ogre of enormous stature with three heads and six arms atop legs as sturdy as tree trunks. He guarded his beautiful red cattle on the island Erythia beyond the setting sun in the stream Oceanus that encircled the world.

Not only did Hercules have to deal with him, there was also a huge dog Orthrus and Eurytion his herdsman. As you might expect, they proved no match for Hercules

but when he began to drive the cattle to his awaiting boat (a huge magical golden cup given to him by the god Helios, with the lion's skin as a sail), Geryon at last was roused from his slumbers and the earth shook as he rushed towards the shore.

Before he could even raise the six weapons he was brandishing, Hercules had loosed three arrows and they found their mark in the three throats of the monster, who was dead before his body hit the ground.

But he crops up again in Dante's Inferno, his soul no doubt finding its way to hell, and he guards the eighth circle, where traitors receive their just desserts. Here he symbolizes fraud, with the face of a just man but the body of a reptile, a huge forked and venomous tail, and tentacles for arms, "hairy to the arm-pits : his back, his breast and both his flanks garish with a variety of knots and whirls".

Hercules doing battle with Geryon. From a kylix by Euphronios and Kachrylion, c. 510 BC

GIANT OCTOPUS

Stories of the Kraken, the monstrous many-armed creature of the deep, that haunted the nightmares of sailors and their families back home, have never been explicit about whether they involved a giant octopus or squid. In the nineteenth century, several giant squids were washed ashore on the coast of Newfoundland and it seemed that the matter had been put to rest.

However, right at the end of the century, in 1896 something very curious indeed turned up on a beach in Florida. The first people to come across it thought it was the rotting carcass of a beached whale, but when a local doctor, an amateur marine biologist in his spare time, was called upon, he pronounced that it was in fact the decaying remains of a giant octopus.

At a conservative estimate he put the weight of the body at about five tons and when he dug around it, he found parts of the tentacles, some of which were over thirty feet long.

Not long afterwards, the putrefying carcass, which must have been hellish to work around, was swept away by a violent storm, but

not before Dr. Webb had photographed it and removed some samples which he sent to Yale University and the Smithsonian Institution in Washington, D.C, who both declared them to be blubber from a whale.

There the matter would have ended if it hadn't been for a scientist called F.G. Wood working in the Ocean Sciences Department of the Naval Undersea Research and Development Laboratory in California in the 1950s.

By chance he came across the story, and, intrigued, he eventually managed to locate one of the specimens.

When he first examined it, he found that although it had been kept in formaldehyde, it was too far gone to reveal anything conclusive about the cellular structure. However it soon became apparent that this was typical of squids and octopuses stored in the same way, but not typical of whale tissue.

Then he noticed that under polarised light, squid and octopus tissue looked completely different. When he went back to his sample, what he saw convinced him that he was looking at a small piece of an absolutely enormous octopus, possibly as much as two hundred feet across from the end of one tip to another.

This is larger by far than the largest squid ever measured. Such a gigantic creature may have remained in the realm of myth and

escaped scientific notice for so long, because like other octopuses, it would spend its life on the ocean floor, waiting to ambush its prey.

Tales of giant octopuses are particularly prevalent in the Bahamas, and this may have been the home of the creature that washed up on the beach, because the currents sweep up from that part of the Caribbean to the coasts of Florida.

Fortunately none of these tales tell of a creature that shows any interest in boats.

GIANTS

According to classical myths, the giants sprang from the blood that spattered the earth when Cronus cut off the genitals of Uranus with a sickle. They were monstrous creations of incredible size and strength, merciless and voracious in their appetites.

Although usually referred to as a race, several are individually named. Tityus for example was one of the four sinners punished in Hades for all eternity. The son of Zeus and Elara, he seemed to have sprung from the earth because Zeus hid the pregnant Elara below ground to protect her from the vengeful jealousy of Hera. When he attempted to ravish Leto on her way from Phocis to Delphi, her sons Apollo and Artemis killed him with arrows from their bows. His punishment was similar to that of Prometheus, being staked to the ground with two vultures either side pecking at his liver, which regrew once it was devoured.

Legends also tell of a famous battle between the gods and the giants, provoked by Gaia who was angry that Zeus had impris- oned her children, the Titans, in Tartarus, a foul infernal place, the same depth below the surface of

the earth as the earth was beneath the heavens.
According to an ancient prophesy, the gods would not prevail without the aid of a mortal so when the giants began hurling enormous boulders and trees engulfed in flames at the heavens, Athena sought out the strongest of all men, Hercules.

He felled Alcyoneus with a volley of arrows but the giant was restored to life when he fell on Gaia, the earth mother who bore him, so Hercules dragged him beyond Pallene where she could not aid him and so he died.

Zeus maddened Porphyrion with the desire for Hera and when he tried to rape her, thunderbolts ands arrows rained down on him. Ephialtes got an arrow from Hercules in his right eye and one from Apollo in his left.

The Fates slew Agrius and Thoas with bronze clubs and Poseidon broke away a piece of the island of Cos and hammered it down on top of Polybotes, making what is now called the island of Nisyros. Mimas died an agonising death pierced by red hot missiles forged by the metalworking god Hepha-

estus and Pallas met his match in the wrathful god of war Athena, who flayed him and used his skin to make an invulnerable shield. She also met Enceladus in battle and crushed him beneath the island of Sicily.

Virgil writes of his body, burnt by thunderbolts, the great mass of mighty Etna pressing down on him, and each time he tries in vain to stand, the whole of Sicily quakes and growls and blackens the sky with smoke.

Orion the hunter was also a giant, killed by a huge scorpion sent by Gaia to thwart his boastful claim that he would not stop hunting until he had killed the last remaining animal on earth.

To punish him still further they both became constellations, so that even in death he is pursued across the sky and to this day you can see Orion fearfully setting as Scorpio rises.

GIANT SQUID

Ever since man first put out to sea, sailors have brought home stories of huge monsters that emerged from the deep and tried to drag their ship down to a watery grave beneath the waves. Perhaps the two most famous examples in literature are the colossal white whale in "Moby Dick" by Hermann Melville and the giant squid in Jules Verne's "Twenty thousand Leagues under the Sea".

For many centuries these stories were told and some of them were believed but they could never be verified, although that did not stop them finding their way into works such as "The Natural History of Norway" by Bishop Erik Ludvigen Pontoppidan written in 1752. He described a many-armed creature, known as the Kraken, that was so large it was often mistaken for an island.

Another naturalist interested in this phenomenon was Denys de Montfort, who was told by American whalers, whom he met in the port of Dunkirk, that they had once hauled aboard something that at first sight appeared to be a fifty foot long sea serpent but which was in fact the tentacle of a giant squid or octopus.

Because the octopus keeps to the sea-bed, waiting in ambush for its prey, anything encountered by a ship on the surface is more likely to be a squid, which is an aggressive predator that goes in search of its prey, propelling itself forward by squirting out jets of water.

However De Montfort did his reputation little favor by a tendency towards exaggeration, describing the giant squid as "the most enormous animals that exist on the globe" without any formal proof whatsoever and it wasn't until long after his death that he was shown to have been on the right track, although of course the blue whale is probably the largest animal ever to have lived.

In 1853 a Danish zoologist, more prone to err on the side of caution, came across pieces of a giant squid, cut from a specimen that was beached on the coast of Denmark.
In 1861 a French gunboat had tried to capture a huge beast, by using their anchor to winch it aboard, but the weight was such that the rope broke and the creature escaped.
In 1878, two fishermen spotted what they thought was a boat that had become stranded in the shallows off the coast of Newfoundland. When they went to its aid, "to their horror [they] found themselves close to a huge fish, having large glassy eyes, which was making desperate efforts to escape, and churning the water into foam by the motions of its immense arms and tail."

With considerable pluck, nay foolhardiness, they netted the thing and towed it ashore, where they tied a line to a tree to prevent it from pulling itself back into the water.
It was an incredible fifty-five feet long, arms and body included.
But modern-day cryptozoologists have pointed at the scars that have been found on the bodies of some whales. These scars are consistent with the marks made on smaller fish by suckers, but their size indicates a squid almost a hundred feet in length, weighing over sixty tons.
Such an animal could well have tried and even succeeded to overwhelm a boat and drag it down to Davy Jones' locker.

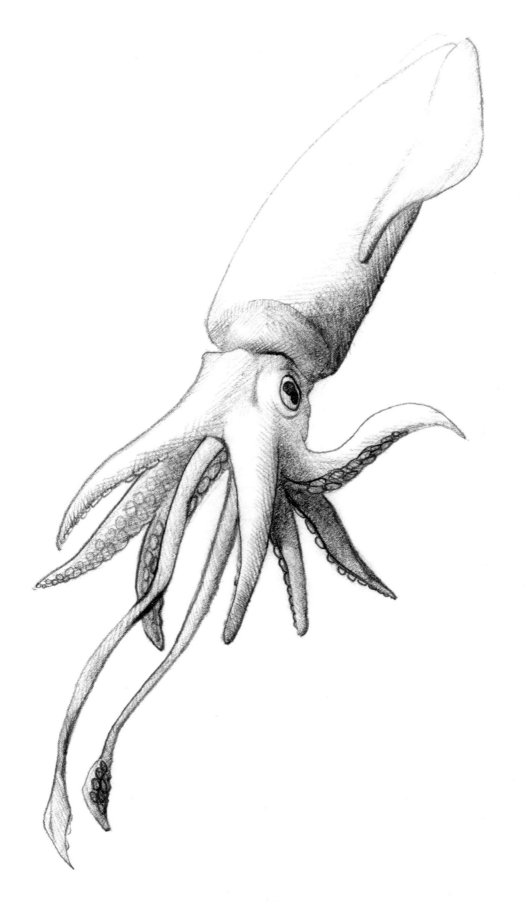

GNOME

Gnomes are small usually bearded creatures, similar in appearance to leprechauns, with pointed caps and buckled shoes. The earth is their native element and they lead a subterranean existence, tunnelling underground, mining precious metals. It is even said that they can move through the earth as easily as we move through the air. In some traditions they become petrified by sunlight during the day, in others they turn into toads or toadstools.

In their realms far beneath the surface they store vast quantities of buried treasure, although some traditions equate this treasure with esoteric knowledge, hence the derivation of the word "gnome" meaning aphorism or maxim from the Greek "gignosko", "to know". Gnomes still feature widely in children's literature and in fantasy role-playing games but once they were taken very seriously. In Iceland roads were diverted to avoid disturbing their habitat.

Nowadays they have become trivialized and debased in such ironic creations as garden gnomes and the smurfs.

GOBLIN

There is some disagreement as to whether goblins are a distinct breed of sprite or rather the malevolent aspect of elves and fairies once their anger is roused. Hence a normally amoral and impulsive sprite although troublesome and mischievous may become disfigured by rage if cheated or otherwise crossed by a mortal and his behaviour will seem monstrous and truly evil.

The school that favors a separate type of imp describes a creature of dwarfish height, responsible for nightmares, spinning them from gossamer and blowing them into the ears of sleeping children. They are shape-shifters able to assume any form to deceive humans, often appearing as long-lost loved ones or favorite pets. They also love to ride horses, stealing them from their stables, and riding them mercilessly throughout the night, returning them in the morning, half-dead and totally unit for work.

Because they cannot nurse their own young, they often steal babies and replace them with their own so they can take the breast milk. Although they do their best with goblin magic to make the baby look human, the mother will usually be able to tell that something is not quite right.

They are also fond of kidnapping women and children, taking them away to their subterranean

kingdoms, sometimes simply out of spite.

The modern concept of goblins owes much to Tolkien's reinvention of them in "The Hobbit"

and they are a common enemy in computer games and role-playing fantasies. They are normally green and hairless although some may have long unkempt greasy locks. At times they are lazy, incompe-

GOBLIN

CONTINUED

tent and easily outwitted, at others cruel and cunning, often aligned to a sorcerer as his foot soldiers and workers of machines of war like siege engines and catapults. The etymology of the word is in dispute. It could be derived from "Gob", the king of the gnomes or alternatively from the Greek word "kobolai" meaning the spirits invoked by rogues.

GOLEM

The word "golem" derives from the Hebrew "gelem" which denotes an unformed substance or raw material. It appears in the bible in Psalm 139, verses 15 and 16.

"My substance was not hid from thee, when as in secret I was made; and in earth's lowest parts was wrought most curiously.

Thine eyes my substance did behold, yet being imperfect; and in the volume of thy book my members all were writ; which after in continuance were fashion'd ever'y one, when as they yet all shapeless were, and of them there was none."

Adam himself was created by God in much the same way that a Jewish rabbi would create a golem.
"And the Lord God formed man of the dust of the ground, and breathed into his nostrils the breath of life, and man became a living soul".

The Talmud describes Adam being "kneaded from a shapeless hunk".

Some golems were created from wood, others from mud and clay, and they were animated by reciting special religious verses or writing the name of God or the word "Emet", meaning "Truth" on their forehead. Supposedly they could be stopped by erasing the first letter in "Emet" to leave "Met" or "Death"

A few rabbis brought forth these creations in secret and their existence was shrouded in mystery. For others it was a sign of their holiness, that they were able in some small way to imitate the generative powers of God. Often in the tales that grew up around the legend of the golem, the rabbi would be punished for striving to play God, and his creation would run amok, turning on its creator. Mary Shelley's Frankenstein is a direct descendant of these morality tales.

But no matter how skilled or holy the rabbi, his creation would never approach the wonders of God's handiwork and golems were always dull and mute shuffling creatures, more like robots than living beings, unable to think for themselves, only able to mindlessly copy or perform repetitive tasks.

were often sightings of strange humanoid creatures.

Gustav Meyrink's "Der Golem" is perhaps the most famous tale of all.

GOLEM

CONTINUED

Many myths arose in the days of the Jewish ghetto, of rabbis creating golems to defend them from persecution and there

"It stalks through the ghetto with a queer groping, stumbling kind of gait, as if afraid of falling over, and quite suddenly is gone. Usually it is seen to disappear round a corner. At other times it is said to have described a circle and gone back to the point where it started-an old house, close by the synagogue".

GORGON

According to Hesiod, there were three gorgons, Stheno (the mighty one), Euryale (the wanderer) and Medusa (the queen). They were the daughters of the Sea god Phorcys and Ceto, although Euripides presents them as the offspring of Gaea the goddess Earth, who bore them to fight by the side of her sons the Titans in their battle against the gods.

Winged creatures with writhing snakes for hair, flat noses, lolling tongues and tusks like wild boars, their ugliness was such that anyone who looked upon them was immediately turned to stone. Of the three, only Medusa was mortal, but the hero Perseus would not have been able to kill her without the help of Athena and Hermes. Hermes gave him his adamantine sickle, which was the only blade that could sever the monster's head. Athena made a gift of her shield, telling Perseus

that he could look at Medusa in the reflection without fear of harm. Then they bade him find the Northern Nymphs, who possessed a cap of darkness which would make him invisible, a magical wallet to carry away the head and shoes that would bear him away on the wind, so he could escape the wrath of the two immortal sisters.

Medusa was pregnant with the children of Poseidon, and so Pegasus and Chrsyaor sprang up

The Gorgon Euryale, depicted on an amphora, 5th century BC.

This he presented to the goddess Athena in recompense for her aid and she wore it on her shield to defeat her enemies.

Hercules was supposed to have asked for a strand of the gorgon's hair from Athena, which he gave to the daughter of the King of Tigea to protect the town from invaders.

GORGON

CONTINUED

from the blood that gushed from the wound when her head was cut from her body.

GRAEA

The Graeae, which literally means "old women" were the three sisters of the gorgons, daughters of Phorcys and Ceto, called Enyo, Pemphredo and Deino. According to Hesiod, they were young and beautiful, only called "old" because they had been born with white hair.

However in the story of Perseus, they are blind and toothless old hags, with just one eye and one tooth between them.

When they were unwilling to help him in his quest to bring back Medusa's head, he stole the eye and tooth to force them to comply with his wishes.

According to Aeschylus, he then consigned the eye and tooth to the bottom of lake Tritonis in Libya.

GRENDEL

The saga of Beowulf tells of the great mead hall of Hrothgar the Danish King, the finest in all Denmark, built to feast and make merry and listen to tall tales in the long dark winter nights.

However misfortune has befallen this hall, for now no man dares stay there after dark, because the beast who lives among the sea inlets and the coastal marshes has been awoken.

"The walker in the shadows, night-stalker, the man-wolf", Grendel is the creature's name and the first night he came prowling around the hall, drawn by the sound of music and laughter, thirty of Hrothgar's retinue who had slept there were slain and all that remained of them were splashes of blood up the wall and pools of blood on the floor.

And night after night, this hideous troll returned until all the bravest warriors had met a similarly gruesome fate.

Beowulf, the nephew of the king of Geatas, in southern Sweden, sails to Denmark with fourteen of his friends to repay a debt owed to Hrothgar by his father. An immensely strong man, he has the strength of thirty champions in his arms and begs the king to allow him to sleep in the hall the night of his arrival.

As the embers in the fireplace die, he watches as one by one his men fall asleep, the mead and the weariness of a long journey getting the better of their fear. They sleep with their swords and shields clutched tight in their arms, but Beowulf knows that no weapon of mortal man can prevail against this monster. He lays aside his armor and his great battleaxe and waits for the fell beast.

Suddenly the huge doors, bolted form the inside with a great beam, burst asunder and in the dark, Beowulf can only make out two deathly pale green eyes flashing with evil intent.

The monster grabs one of the champions and rips him limb from limb, draining the warm blood, and then he reaches out for another to slake his thirst and finds his own arm caught in a grip such as he has never felt before. And then for the first time he knows fear. Gathering round the wrestling figures, rolling and crashing and writhing on the ground, the champions triy to strike at the troll but so tightly locked are the pair, that they have difficulty aiming their blows and when they do succeed, their swords bounce off the scales of the troll's back like drumsticks off a drum, and then they realize they must let fate decide who will win this battle.

As Grendel grows wearier and wearier, for he has never met a foe who was his match, he becomes more and more desperate to free himself from this great bear-like grip until he wrenches free by tearing his own arm off at the shoulder and then he runs screaming back to the foul marshes whence he came.

There is much feasting that night in the hall, the mead flows, the valor of the hero is toasted over and over again, however little do they know their troubles are only just beginning for Grendel has run back to his cave and died in his mother's arms and her thirst for revenge makes her altogether more fearsome than her son. But that is another story.

COLOR

SECTION

Chimera, Pegasus &
Bellerophon

Phoenix

Jinn

Troll

Griffin

Cyclops

Dragon

Fairies, Elves & Sprites

Unicorn

Giant Octopus

Sea Serpent

Werewolf

Zombie

Vampire

Minotaur

Medusa

CREATURES

G TO Z

GRIFFIN

Griffins are chimerical creatures with the legs and body of a lion and the head and wings of an eagle. Depending on whom you believe, their diet consisted principally either of horses or of men. Pausanias wrote of their treasures of gold, which they constantly

guarded against their greedy and grasping neighbors, the Arimaspians.

The origins of the legend probably lie in the Orient, as historians have uncovered reports of people arriving in Rome from Central Asia, supposedly having fled the clutches of these ravening beasts. Other writers claim that they come from the North, right on the edge of the world, beyond the North Wind, where the Hyperboreans lived.

For a while scholars thought the legend originated with the Scythians, amongst whose art the griffin features heavily, but the theory has not been widely accepted, for the griffin was also popular in ancient Greek and Cretan art and architecture.

There were huge griffins painted on the walls of the throne room in the palace of Minos so as well as being predatory it could have

had some protective virtues. Sometimes it was even shown as the victims of larger more powerful beasts.

It could be found on tombs and in temples, either recumbent or sitting up, often opposite a sphinx. As it evolved, it was also shown with its beak open, over a sinuous tongue and with the ears of a horse and gradually two distinct types evolved, the Greek and the Asiatic, the former with a curly mane and the latter with a crest on top of its head.

As was the case with many other mythical monsters, there was a thriving market for griffin fossils, such as claws, which were usually either the tusks or horns of mammoths and wooly rhinoceroses, and sometimes the antlers of antelopes.

HARPY

The word "harpies" comes from the Greek "harpyia", meaning "snatchers". They were the daughters of Thaumas and Electra, who were respectively the son of Pontus the Sea and the daughter of Oceanus. Hence it is probable that they personified the strong winds that snatch sailors away to their misfortune or death. They were also seen as souls of the dead that snatch away the souls of the living, and as such they were often represented as birds with the faces of cruel and ugly women.

In one incident they were supposed to have borne away two sisters, both under the protection of Aphrodite, to give to the Erinyes as slaves. In another they were sent to the court of King Phineus in Thrace as punishment for the way he treated his children. If Calais and Zetes, the sons of Boreas, had not chased them away, the harpies' disgusting habits of stealing and spoiling the food would have led to widespread starvation.

The names of four harpies are known: Podarge (swift foot), Aello (storm wind), Ocypete (swift wing), and Calaeno which means "dark". You can see what they looked like on the "harpy tomb" in the British Museum, discovered in Xanthus in Lycia.

HIND OF CERYNEIA

There are several different versions of the story of the hind of Ceryneia, which Hercules had to capture for his third task.

According to the Greek scholar Apollodorus, who collected many of the Greek myths in his "Bibliotheca", it took Hercules a whole year to catch the hind, so fleet of foot was it, eventually stopping it with an arrow as it was on the point of crossing the river Ladon in Arcadia. Then he carried it alive to King Eurystheus.

On his long journey, he met Apollo and Artemis, to whom the deer was sacred. Greatly angered to see it so brutally treated, she wanted to take it back, but relented on hearing of his arduous labors.

Euripides concludes the task with the hind being mortally wounded by Hercules' arrow. Pindar has the chase ending in the extreme northern limits of the world, the land of the Hyperboreans.

It is possible that the hind became sacred to Artemis after one of the Pleiades, the seven sisters immortalized in the constellation, was turned into a deer by Artemis, to escape the amorous clutches of Zeus.

The Greek poet Callimachus tells of five hinds of enormous size with horns of gold, four of which were captured by Artemis, to pull her chariot, the fifth escaping and finding its way to Mount Ceryneia, hence the name.

Hercules and the Hind of Ceryneia, from a cup 480 BC

hippogriff

"When mare and griffin meet and mate
Their offspring share a curious fate
One half is horse with hooves and tail
The rest is eagle, claws and nail.

As a horse it like to graze
In summer meadows doused with haze
Yet as an eagle it can fly
Above the clouds where dreams drift by.
With such a beast I am enthralled
The hippogriff this beast is called."

As this poem by Arnold Sundgaard reveals, the hippogriff was a very curious creature to behold. A product of the union between a mare and a male griffin, it had an eagle's head, beak, talons and feathered wings but the body of a horse.

What is particularly strange is that griffins were said to hate horses, sometimes even preying on them and therefore the chance of a pair mating was so rare as to have become emblematic of the impossible and the ability of love to conquer all.

The offspring of such an unlikely coupling was an omnivore and far less intractable than its sire, making an excellent steed for wizards and knights, able to fly as fast a bolt of thunder.

HORSE OF DIOMEDES

According to legend, Diomedes, the king of the Bistones, a fierce tribe from Thrace, kept four mares, which were so aggressive, they had to be chained to their stables with iron and bronze collars. Their hunger was such that it could only be cured with raw human flesh.

For his eighth labor, Hercules was sent to steal them, and in the process he paid Diomedes back for his barbarism by feeding him to his own horses.

King Eurystheus used them to breed from, and the bloodline was supposed to have continued to the days of Alexander the Great. Apollodorus changes the story slightly, making Hercules drive the horses down to the sea, then turning to deal with the Bistones, who had been roused by the sound of fighting in the stables.

His lover, Abderus, was killed by the horses as Hercules fended off the wild men and in his honor he founded the city of Abdera.

In this version Eurystheus releases the horses and they make their way to Mount Olympus where they are killed by ravenous beasts.

hundred handers

The hundred-handers were the brothers of Cronus, pushed back into the womb because their father feared and hated them.

According to Hesiod "they were huge and strong beyond all telling. From their shoulders sprang a hundred arms, terrible to behold, and each had fifty heads upon his shoulders, growing from sturdy bodies. Boundless and powerful was the strength that lay in their mighty forms."

When Cronus freed them from their mother's womb he was also fearful of their power so he imprisoned them in Tartarus and set Campe to guard them.

When Zeus fought Cronus and the other titans, he freed the hundred-handers and they helped him to overcome them, and they in turn were set to guard the titans.

Later, when the gods rebelled against Zeus, the strongest of the three hundred handers, Briareos, came to his aid and intimidated the gods into acquiescence.

HYDRA

The Hydra, like Cerberus, was an offspring of the giant Typhon and Echidna, a monstrous being, half woman half beast. Depending on whom you believe, it had either one hundred heads, nine heads or just the one head. Most sources agree that it had nine heads, eight mortal and one immortal, in the middle.

After he had killed the Nemean Lion, Hercules was commanded by King Eurystheus, to kill the Hydra which haunted the swamps of Lerna, south of Argos.

Hercules was driven in a chariot by Iolaus, the son of his half-brother Iphicles, and as they drew near the air became foul with the poisonous breath emanating from the Hydra's many heads.

Hercules spied its den on the hill beside the spring Amymone and began to shoot at it with his arrows to lure it out.

Maddened by the pinpricks, which stung its hide like insect bites, it burst forth gnashing its terrible teeth. Straightaway Hercules began chopping off its many heads, but to his consternation, two heads sprang up from each severed neck and soon he was in great danger of being overwhelmed.

He urged Iolaus to seal each wound with a burning torch and in this way the heads could not regrow. Soon all the mortal heads were gone and with one last mighty stroke, the immortal head was cleaved from the body. Triumphant Hercules scooped up it up and buried it under a rock on the road from Lerna to Eleaus. He cut open the hydra's foul body and dipped his arrows in the gall.
This was to prove his undoing, for years later, this great man, whom none it seemed could kill, died when his wife, Deianira, smeared the poison on his robe.

The centaur Nessus had tried to carry her off and Hercules shot him with one of these deadly arrowheads.

As he lay dying, he told Deianira, that should her husband's love for her ever wane, it would revive if she rubbed some blood from the wound onto his skin.
When she did this, it is said that his screams of agony could be heard in Mount Olympus.

JABBERWOCKY

'Twas brillig, and the slithy toves
Did gyre and gimble in the wabe;
All mimsy were the borogroves,
And the mome raths outgrabe.

Beware the Jabberwock, my son!
The jaws that bite, the claws that

catch!
Beware the Jubjub bird and shun
The frumious Bandersnatch!

He took his vorpal sword in hand:
Long time the manxome foe he
sought-
So rested he by the Tumtum tree,
And stood awhile in thought.

And as in uffish thought he stood,
The Jabberwock, with eyes of
flame,
Came whiffling through the tulgey
wood,
And burbled as it came!

One two! One two! And through

and though
The vorpal blade went snicker-
snack!
He left it dead, and with its head
He went galumphing back.

"And hast thou slain the Jabber-
wock!
Come to my arms, my beamish
boy!
O frabjious day! Callooh!
Callay!"
He chortled in his joy.

'Twas brillig, and the slithy toves
Did gyre and gimble in the wabe;
All mimsy were the borogroves,
And the mome raths outgrabe.

JINN

One school of thought believes that the word "genie" is borrowed from the Arabic word "jinn". Another school believes it derives from the Latin word "genius" meaning "protective spirit". Whichever is true, "genie" and "jinn" are now to all intents and purposes synonymous.

Before Islam, the jinn were much like the pagan concept of imps and fairies, malevolent super-natural creatures who maddened animals, spoiled crops, drove the weak-minded insane and generally made a nuisance of themselves. They could shape-shift but remained for the most part invisible. Like the European succubi they were responsible for the enervated state and nightly emissions of young men. The word "ghoul" comes form the Arabic "ghul", which was a kind of jinn, as were ifrit and sila.

With the rise of Islam there developed a more complex theory of jinn. It was believed that God made them from fire that gave no smoke, just as man was made from the dust and clay of the earth.

They were beneath angels in the supernatural hierarchy, but unlike angels they had free will and could therefore choose whether or not to follow the will of god. According to the Koran, the devil was not an angel but a jinn.

They lived lives modelled on

human societies and generally ignored us although they were always aware of our existence. Sometimes they took an interest in human affairs or were actively summoned and then they made themselves visible. Sorcerers had to take care to know the jinn they were dealing with, as there were four distinct types aligned to earth, air, fire and water and some were more amenable than others.

To attempt to bind a jinn to one's will was an undertaking fraught with danger. The jinn could take revenge by possessing the sorcerer or cursing him with ill fortune. This could be reversed by reciting special verses from the Koran or appealing to the angel who was responsible for the particular tribe to which the jinn belonged.

widespread belief that certain spells could bind them to man-made objects or places, as was the case with Aladdin's lamp in the tale from "The Thousand and One Nights".

It was said that the Seal of Solomon gave him authority over the jinn and there was a

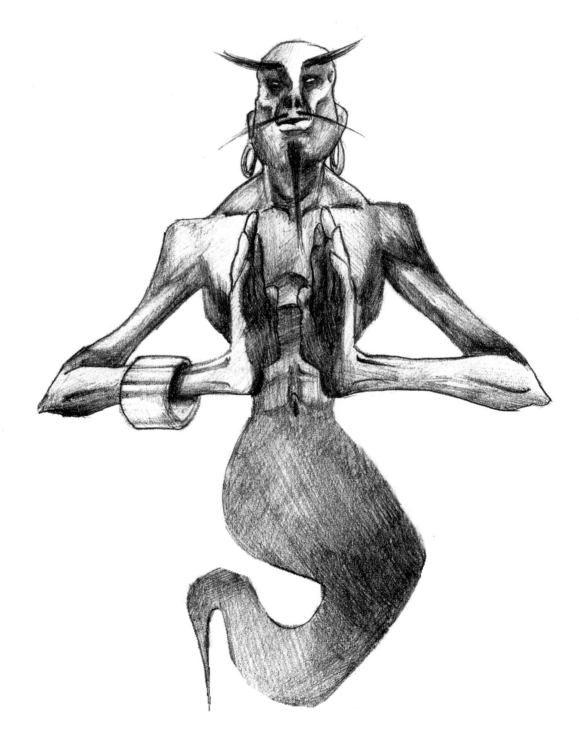

LADON

Ladon was the "fearful serpent" with a hundred heads and a thousand different voices, who, along with the Hesperides, guarded the golden apples at the edge of the world, which Hercules had to steal for his eleventh labour.

This garden is either beyond the setting sun, where Atlas bears the weight of the sky on his shoulders, or towards the northern limits of the earth in the land of the Hyperboreans.

The daughters of Atlas were wont to steal the apples, which were wedding gifts from the Earth Mother to Zeus and Hera, hence the need for a guard. There are several different versions of what happened.

In one, Hercules takes Atlas' burden on to his shoulders for a while, in return for his going to fetch the apples. When Atlas returns, he decides he likes his new-found freedom and will not fulfil his side of the bargain, but Hercules tricks the oafish titan into taking back his burden, pretending that if Atlas will just

L

In another version, Hercules kills Ladon himself with his arrows, and the poison of the hydra is too much for the serpent. So deadly indeed is this poison that the flies which settle on the wounds shrivel and die.

In return for helping the Hesper-ides, the singing nymphs, Ladon was made immortal in the heavens as the constellation Draco, where you can see him to this day between Ursa Major and Ursa Minor. However not even in the afterlife can he escape Hercules, who stands over him with his mighty club in his hand.

take the weight for a second, he can put a cushion between his head and the sky.

Of course once the giant has the weight, Hercules never takes it back.

LAESTRYGONIANS

When Odysseus found a sheltered cove at Telepylus to rest his weary men, he did not bank on meeting the Laestrygonians, giant cannibals who lived nearby.

Making fast his ship to the mouth of the naturally formed harbour, he sent three scouts to explore the land and they soon met a strapping young girl drawing water not far from a village. Claiming to be the daughter of King Antiphates, she led them back to his palace, where they met an even taller woman, the King's wife. So large and ugly was she, that they immediately fell back in horror but before they knew what was happening, the enormous king was already upon them and he snatched one of them up and began to eat him.

Running for their lives, the two other scouts returned to the ships with the giants in hot pursuit. Only Odysseus' ship managed to escape, the giants smashing the rest of the fleet with boulders and spearing the men like fish, taking them back to feast on their flesh.

The Laestrygonians destroying Odysseus' fleet, from a cave painting circa 100 BC.

LEPRECHAUN

In the pecking order of mythological creatures, leprechauns occupy a position somewhere between fairies and pixies, more benevolent than the latter, more willing to communicate with mortals than the former. Nevertheless they are not altogether to be trusted and their wisdom and advice may prove to be misleading and self-defeating. It is also almost impossible to wrest from them the whereabouts of their crock of gold. Often they will part with something that looks like gold but fades away after a short time.

The derivation of the word is thought to lie in the old Irish word "luchorpan", "lu" meaning "small" and "corp" meaning "body" but it could also come from "luprachan" meaning "half-embodied", hinting at their supernatural origins, belonging fully neither to the physical nor to the spiritual realms.

For some reason the leprechaun has become associated with cobblers and his expertise with shoe repairs is legendary.

Most modern representations show a little old man with a beard and a pipe, a clog on his lap and a mouthful of nails, busily hammering away, wearing a tam o' shanter, leather apron and emerald green jacket. He almost always has silver buckles on his shoes, and his purse by his side with the shilling piece that magically reappears when spent.

LEVIATHAN

Leviathan is a creature shrouded in mystery and speculation. The only description we have to go on, comes from a lengthy passage in the bible that is not actually very helpful when trying to build up a picture of what leviathan is supposed to look like.
Here is the passage from the book of Job, with a few cuts.

"Canst thou draw out leviathan with an hook? Or his tongue with a cord which thou lettest down?

Canst thou put an hook into his nose or bore his jaw through with a thorn? Will he make many supplications unto thee? Will he speak soft words unto thee? Will he make a covenant thee? Wilt thou take him for a servant forever? Wilt thou play with him as with a bird? Or wilt thou bind him for thy maidens? Shall the companions make a banquet of him? Shall they part him among the merchants?

"Canst thou fill his skin with barbed irons? Or his head with fish spears? Lay thine hand upon him, remember the battle, do no more. Behold the hope of him is in vain: shall not one be cast down even at the sight of him? None is so fierce that dare stir him up: who then is able to stand before me?

Who can open the doors of his face? His teeth are terrible round about. His scales are his pride, shut up together as with a close seal. One is so near to another, that no air can come between them. They are joined one to another, they stick together, that they cannot be sundered.

"By his neesings (sneezing!) a light doth shine, and his eyes are like the eyelids of the morning. Out of his mouth go burning lamps, and sparks of fire leap out. Out of his nostrils goeth smoke as out of a seething pot or caldron. His breath kindleth coals, and a flame goeth out of his mouth. "In his neck remaineth strength, and sorrow is turned into joy before him. The flakes of his flesh

are joined together : they are firm in themselves : they cannot be moved. His heart is as firm as a stone; yea as hard as a piece of the nether millstone.

"When he raiseth up himself, the mighty are afraid : by reason of breakings they purify themselves. The sword of him that layeth at him cannot hold : the spear, the dart, nor the habergeon. He esteemeth iron as straw, and brass as rotten wood. The arrow cannot make him flee: slingstones are turned with him into stubble. Darts are counted as stubble: he laugheth at the shaking of a spear. Sharp stones are under him: he spreadeth sharp pointed things upon the mire.

"He maketh the deep boil like a pot: he maketh the sea like a pot of ointment. He maketh a path to shine after him: one would think the deep to be hoary.

"Upon the earth there is not his like, who is made without fear. He beholdeth all high things: he is a king over all the children of pride."

I quote from the King James translation, because it is so rich and poetical in its language, although sometimes, as in this case, it can be rather unclear to our modern ears. However if you read the passage in the Revised Standard Version or the New English Bible you would be none the wiser. If you can picture to yourself a clear image of leviathan you are a better man than I am.

I would have said from the scales and teeth that it resembles the Nile crocodile. The fire-breathing nostrils are probably not meant to be taken literally. Instead they convey an impression of ferocity. However another passage from Psalm 104 confuses the issue still further.

"So is this great and spacious sea, wherein things creeping are, which number'd cannot be; and beasts both great and small are there. There ships go; there thou mak'st to play that leviathan great."

This is clearly referring to some ocean-going animal, and only the estuary crocodiles of SE Asia and Australia venture out to sea. It is possible that in this context the word leviathan is used to describe a whale.

LOCH NESS MONSTER

Perhaps the most famous of all mythical creatures is the Loch Ness monster. The legend of

Nessie, as he or rather she is fondly known, possesses all the ingredients of the best monster myths-the sightings, the teasingly inconclusive photographic evidence, the remoteness and extent of her territory that could just possibly hide an animal that is supposed to have been extinct for millions of years and the tantalizing result that her existence while not yet proven, cannot be disproven.

Loch Ness is an enormous body of water, twenty-four miles long, in places over a mile wide, and nearly a thousand feet deep. Below a certain depth it can become very gloomy, with almost no visibility and there are underwater currents which make diving dangerous.

If you look at that part of Scotland on a map you will notice that the loch is in a cleft which cuts the

country in two. Millions of years ago, Loch Ness was part of the sea, before the land shifted and fenced it in, although a river still runs from the loch to the North Sea.

This is what has led scientists to investigate what would otherwise be considered the wild claims of drunken or conniving Scotsmen. Is it possible that some kind of marine creature has become trapped there?

Tales had always been told of a creature that lived in Loch Ness, but it wasn't until 1933 when a road was built around it that people actually claimed to have seen the creature. Many of the sightings were from drivers passing the loch, the first being Mr. and Mrs. Mackay in April of that same year, who described "an enormous animal" that "disported itself, rolling and plunging for fully a minute."
It must be borne in mind, that Mr. and Mrs. Mackay owned a hotel nearby and would therefore stand to benefit from an influx of tourists to the area.

A friend of theirs, Alex Campbell, who oversaw the local salmon fishing also claimed to have seen the monster and he wrote about it in the Inverness Courier.
"It had a long, tapering neck, about six feet long and a smallish head with a serpentine look about it, and a huge hump behind, which I reckoned was about thirty feet long."

The next year a young student,

Arthur Grant burst into his house one evening swearing that he had nearly run the thing over on his motorbike as he rode home. His description matched Campbell's, and he made a sketch, which palaeontologists recognized as a plesiosaurus.

In Spring of the same year, the famous photograph was taken by the "London Surgeon" vacationing by the loch, who remained nameless until after his death. The photograph, although at first sight compelling, presents several problems.

For a start there is nothing to show that it was taken at Loch Ness, as it is made up only of a stretch of water and the peculiar projection from the surface. This also means that there is nothing to judge the scale of the object. Lastly, the object is cast in shadow, so it could be anything, such as a log or a diving bird.

The next piece of evidence is the film footage taken by Tim Dinsdale in 1960. This has also been the subject of much controversy. It is distinctly unimpressive, just a black spot moving in the distance. Some say that it could be a speedboat, others cite the photographic specialists of the RAF who speculate that it could be almost a hundred feet long.

There were however those in the scientific community who took the eyewitness statements and the footage seriously enough to launch a proper investigation and before long they too had their

own footage but once again it was impossible to state unequivocally that this was evidence of a hitherto unidentified species of marine animal.

One underwater photograph shows what may be a flipper about eight feet long. Another could be the face of the Loch Ness monster. There is also a shot taken of a creature with a long neck swimming away from the camera. In all cases the murkiness of the water prevents absolute verifica-

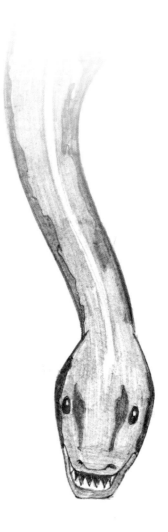

LOCH NESS MONSTER CONTINUED

tion.

Of course, if there is a Loch Ness monster, there must be more than one. And this raises the question of whether there is enough food in the loch to sustain a breeding population of large carnivores. The answer appears to be that there is enough salmon, unfortunately the loch is so big that it is not possible to deduce from the numbers whether they are being drastically predated.

So what kind of animal could Nessie be? Well, the most popular choice is the plesiosaurus, which fits all the descriptions given by the eyewitnesses, but as this is a cold-blooded reptile it could not survive the extremely cold waters of the loch. Some research however seems to suggest that ancient reptiles may have been able to regulate their body temperature, in much the same way that mammals do.

It has also been postulated that Nessie is a primitive whale or a giant otter, a species of which does exist in the Amazon River. But both of these theories come unstuck when you consider that, as mammals which need to come to the surface to breathe, they should be spotted every few minutes not every few years. Could it be some kind of giant slug that would sink to the bottom and leave no skeletal evidence? Could there be a tunnel connecting Loch Ness to the sea or to an even bigger loch underground? Whatever answer you prefer, it seems that the dark and murky waters are not going to give up their secrets for a long time and we must accept the possibility that the mystery may never be solved.

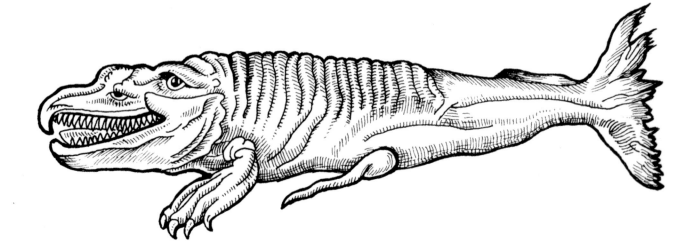

MANTICORE

The word manticore derives from a misspelling of the word "marticoras" which itself derives from the Persian "martya" meaning "man" and "xvar", "to eat".

When Pliny the Elder was writing "Naturalis Historia", his copy of Aristotle's work on natural history from which he drew his information on this fabulous beast, contained several errors.

The Greeks first learned of the manticore from Ctesias who himself heard of it at the court of King Artxerxes II in Persia.

Rumors abounded of a fearsome animal that lurked in the jungles of India, which was as big as a horse with the body of a lion and the face of a man, with three tiered rows of iron teeth and the tail of a dragon that could shoot out poisonous hairs like darts. The writer Pausanias was inclined to think that this strange creature was in fact the tiger, which he had seen in the arena at Rome. He knew that the very real dread

this animal inspired in the Indians made it the subject of exaggeration and distortion.

During the sixteenth century it was often used by artists to represent the sin of fraud which had an appealing face on the body of a vile beast, and in paintings it closely resembles the sphinx.

To this day the myth endures and whenever someone disappears in the forests of Indonesia, he is said to have fallen victim to the manticore, which always completely devours his prey, leaving no trace.

MERMAID

The concept of mermaids and mermen in ancient civilizations is very widespread and may stem from the even older fish-tailed gods which permeated the beliefs of Japanese, Greek, Chinese, Indian and Native American cultures, the last of which speaks of a mysterious half-man-half-fish who led their ancestors from Asia to America.

The oldest fish god is Oannes, Lord of the Ocean, who was worshipped by the Sumerians about 7000 years ago when civilization as we understand it today began. The Greek Tritons and Sirens and the Phoenician Dagon were also human from the waist up and fish below.

It is thought that sightings of seals, which often sit vertically in the water to look about, and from afar can look remarkably human, gave rise to the modern myth.

There is a direct link between the two in the Norwegian and Hebridean legends of the seal-maids who would come ashore and remove their seal-skins to bask in the sun. If their seal-skins were stolen they could not return to the sea and there are many stories of men making wives for themselves of these seal-maids by hiding their skins, only to come back one day from fishing to find the skin has been discovered and wife has returned to her kin to play beneath the waves.

Mermaids were likened to the fairies in that they had no soul and although not immortal they lived for many more years than men. They were also very fond of music and their singing haunted the dreams of sailors. This in itself may have begun with tales

of whale songs, which make the hulls of wooden ships hum and vibrate.

Sometimes mermaids would make predictions, and offer gifts to men, which usually had disastrous consequences. If they were crossed or ill-used their revenge would always be cruel, bringing floods and wrecking ships.

Although there were sometimes marriages between mermaids and men, they never went well. The relationship would inevitably have started in bad faith by the mortal stealing something like a comb or

mirror and thus gaining control over her, and the mermaid would never stop yearning for the sea. In stories like "Melusine" and "The Lady of Lyn y Fan Fach", the marriage begins with a compact and as soon as it is broken, the mermaid returns to the sea forever.

In fact contact with mermaids was normally avoided, as sailors who saw one from their ship were doomed to die at sea, never again

to see their families.

Sometimes mermaids bewitched men and turned them away from their kind to live with them under the waves.

From the following report of a documented sighting in 1608 one can only presume the crew were drunk or lying or both.

"This morning one of our company looking overboard saw a mermaid, and calling up some of the company to see her, one more came up, and by the time she was come close to the ship's side,

looking earnestly on the men, a sea came and overturned her. From the navel upward her back and breasts were like a woman's, her body as big as one of us, her skin very white and long hair hanging down behind, of the color black. In her going down they saw her tail, which was like the tail of a porpoise and speckled like a mackerel."

Next we have an excerpt from an article taken from a Boston

newspaper as recently as 1881, relating a journalist's experience of seeing a preserved mermaid at first hand.

"This wonder of the deep is in a fine state of preservation. The head and body of a woman are very plainly and distinctly marked. The features of the face, eyes, nose, mouth, teeth, arms, breasts and hair are those of a human being. The hair on its head is of a pale silky blonde, several inches in length. The arms terminate in claws closely resembling an eagle's talons instead of fingers with nails. From the waist up, the resemblance to a woman is perfect, and from the waist down, the body is exactly the same as the ordinary mullet of our waters, with its scales, fins and tail."

This was undoubtedly one of the many fakes that were doing the rounds and by all accounts making the fraudsters incredibly rich. Unlike the beautiful mermaids that win the hearts of princes in fairy tales such as "The Little Mermaid" by Hans Christian Anderson these specimens were incredibly ugly, because they were often shaved monkeys stitched onto the tail of a fish. Sometimes orang-utans and dolphin tails were used to make exhibits of a more impressive size.

MINOTAUR

The Minotaur was a huge man of enormous strength with a great bull's head atop his shoulders. His mother was Queen Pasiphae, the wife of King Minos the second of Crete. And his father...

Well, King Minos had been a very arrogant man, claiming that he received his right to rule direct from the gods and to prove it he boasted that whatever he prayed for would come true. He asked for Poseidon to send him a bull from the sea, promising to sacrifice it to the god. But when the bull duly appeared, he thought it was too fine a beast to waste and he sacrificed one of his own instead. This greatly angered Poseidon who made his wife fall head-over-heels in love with the bull as punishment for his unworthy behavior. Daedalus, who had fled Athens for Crete, charged with murder, designed a wooden frame in the shape of a cow, covered in hide, in which Pasiphae concealed herself, and thus she was able to consummate her love for the bull.

On discovering the frightful progeny of this unnatural union, King Minos hid the Minotaur in the labyrinth, which had been built by Daedalus, and threw him in jail.

Such was the impenetrable nature of this tortuously winding maze, that King Minos knew the Minotaur would never escape but he could not quite bring himself to abandon him to starvation, he was his stepson after all.

So every year he demanded tribute from the Athenians, whom he had conquered in battle, of

seven young men and seven young women who would sail to Crete and enter the lair of the Minotaur as his prey.
 The mere mention of his name struck fear into the heart of every Athenian boy and girl as lots were drawn to see who would make the final voyage to meet this terrible fate.

In the third year it fell to Theseus to join the ship sailing to Crete. Fortunately for Theseus, he was a very handsome young man and Ariadne, the daughter of King Minos, promptly fell in love with him. In return for his promising to take her away with him, she asked Daedalus to show her how one could escape from the labyrinth. He advised her to give Theseus a

ball of wool and then nail one end to the doorway and pay out the thread as he made his way in. She armed Theseus with a sword and waited outside with her heart in her mouth.

 It must have been a mighty battle indeed for Theseus was a great warrior, strong of arm and stout

of heart and very skilled with a
sword. Eventually he did manage
to overcome the fell beast and he
cut off his head for all to see that
his reign of terror was at an end.

MOTHMAN

Late one cold and dark November night, back in 1967, two teenaged couples from Point Pleasant West Virginia, who had been necking in a popular lovers' lane outside town, were driving home past the abandoned munitions dump, when they saw something very strange. Outside the empty power plant was a dark figure, "shaped like a man but bigger". Caught in the light of the car's beams, the figure looked as though it had wings folded behind its back, and its eyes blazed as though lit from within.

Naturally enough, the kids were seized with the desire to get out of the deserted gloomy area, back to the lights and familiar streets of their hometown.

On the way, driving faster than usual, they discussed what it could have been, and they had just about convinced themselves that it was a trick of the light, just a shadow, when they suddenly saw that the creature, with wings unfurled, was flying alongside the car.

No matter how much the driver gunned the engine, he could not shake the creature off, and it followed them all the way along Route 62, "squawking like a mouse", until they reached the

outskirts of town and it flew off into the night.

Although a search of the area by the sheriff's deputies proved fruitless, the story hit the papers the next day, and the creature, which was first described simply as "The Bird", soon came to be known by the rather more illustrious title of "Mothman".

Naturally enough, one sighting was followed by another. This time, a young mother, her baby and two friends were visiting a couple near the munitions dump. She describes seeing it as she emerged from the car.

"It seemed as if it had been lying down. It rose slowly from the ground. A big grey thing. Bigger than a man, with terrible glowing eyes."

One detail that lends credence to what might otherwise seem a rather unconvincing story is that she was so frightened she dropped her baby.

The couple helped her gather it up and together they ran for the house, locking themselves inside and listening as the creature approached the house with a slow shuffling gait and tried to peer in at the window.

This second appearance sparked a whole series, some of them obviously hoaxes, others the product of an overactive imagination, but the uniformity of many of the descriptions (grey, standing between six and seven feet tall, with a wingspan of ten feet), leads one to suspect that something very out of the ordinary was going on.

Connie Carpenter was driving home one night when the creature flew right at her car, forcing her to swerve. Because it came so near, right in the light of her full beams, she got probably the closest look at its face.

"Those eyes were very red and once they were fixed on me I couldn't take my own eyes off them. It's a wonder I didn't have a wreck. [The face] was horrible... like something out of a science-fiction movie."

There have been several attempts to explain the Mothman mystery. One suggestion is that the sightings were of the rare sandhill crane, which is tall and grey with a waxy red forehead. According to Dr. Robert Smith, professor of biology at West Virginia University, the bird is aggressively territorial and may well have flown at passing cars.

Perhaps the most eerie explanation is that Mothman was a portent of disaster, such as the comets or sea serpents that were thought to presage cataclysmic events in the Middle Ages.

About a year after the first sightings, a suspension bridge over the Ohio River near Point Pleasant collapsed, tipping the heavy rush hour traffic into the freezing water below. Fifty people died and Mothman was never seen again.

MUMMY

The mummy that comes to life and emerges from its coffin, bandages trailing, arms outstretched, to pursue the archeologist who has inadvertently disturbed its eternal rest, seems like an archetypal image but is actually a modern phenomenon born of the two classic films starring Christopher Lee and Boris Karloff.

The idea of a protective curse threatening a terrible revenge on whosoever desecrates the sacred space of a royal tomb stems from the nineteenth century. Egyptian archaeology itself had begun in the early eighteen hundreds when Napoleon invaded Egypt. The amazing discoveries made by the scholars who accompanied his expedition were sent back to Paris and then found their way to museums and private collections all over Europe.

All the newspapers were full of stories of the colossal statues of the pharaohs and their mysterious royal tombs covered in inscrutable hieroglyphs, filled with fabulous treasures. Naturally this fired the imagination of the writers of the day and Jane Loudon Webb was the first to introduce the idea of the mummy's curse to the literary

cannon with her tale set in the 22nd century about a young scholar whose life is threatened by a vengeful mummy.

This was followed shortly afterwards by the anonymous novel "The Fruits of Enterprise" in which several explorers of an Egyptian pyramid invoke a curse by foolishly setting fire to a mummy to use as a torch in the

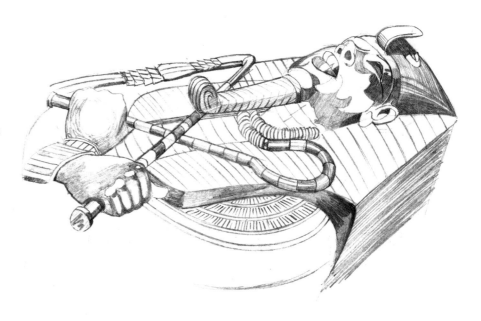

dark underground passages. And then in 1869 Louisa May Alcott, the author of "Little Women" wrote a short story "Lost in a pyramid; or the Mummy's Curse" about some mysterious seeds which an archeologist finds in a coffin and brings home for his fiance, to her eventual undoing.

When the Titanic sank in 1912, tales were told of an unscrupulous antique dealer who had bought a coffin containing the mummy of a prophetess who lived at the court of Amenhotep IV. He dismissed

the rumors of a curse surrounding the mummy but then began to fear the worst when his gun exploded in his hand on the way back to England and his arm had to be amputated at the elbow.

When he arrived home, he found that two of his closest friends and two of his servants had died in freak accidents. Before long his girlfriend and her mother

were suffering from a mysterious wasting disease that ultimately ended in their deaths.

By then he was anxious to be rid of the sarcophagus and he donated it to the British Museum, which was already inundated with Egyptian artifacts so an exchange was made with the Museum of Natural History in New York. Before the shipping arrangements had been finalized, the director of Egyptology and his chief photographer were dead. The ship upon which the mummy eventually

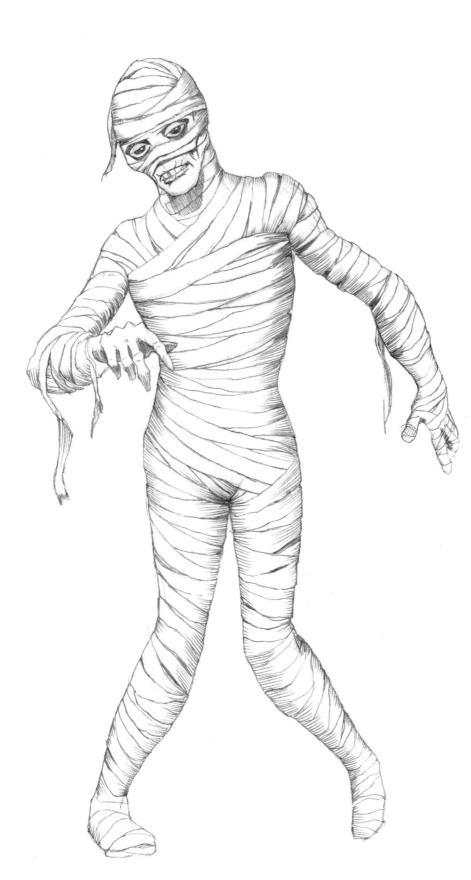

sailed was the Titanic.

When Tutankhamun's burial chamber was discovered in 1922 the author Marie Corelli wrote an article in which she claimed that "the most dire punishment follows any rash intruder into a sealed tomb" and a legend was born. Apocryphal tales were told of an inscription over the entrance that promised "Death shall come on swift wings to him that toucheth the tomb of Pharaoh."

Just seven weeks after the discovery, Lord Carnarvon, who had funded the excavation died in Cairo from an infected mosquito bite. At the exact moment when he expired all the lights in his house in England went out and his dog barked and passed away. The newspapers went mad and "King Tut-mania" gripped the world as the deaths of the other participants in the dig were eagerly awaited.

However the journalists had rather a long wait with the other principal archaeologist, Howard Carter, who died seventeen years later from natural causes.

NEMEAN LION

Some scholars say that the lion's skin, which Hercules wore draped around his shoulders, the scalp over his head like a helmet, belonged to the Nemean lion, which he defeated on the first of his twelve labors. Others contend that it was the skin of a lion he had killed while guarding the cattle of Amphitryon, well before his labors began.

According to the second version, Hercules had been approached by two mysterious women, called Vice and Virtue, one of whom offered him an easy pleasurable life, the other a life of suffering and glory. Just as he chose the latter, he saw a huge lion attacking his herd. It took him many days to find its lair, and but when he did, he laid the beast at his feet with one almighty blow from his stout club.

When he tried to remove the hide to carry back to Thebes as a trophy he found that his knife would not even make a mark on the thick pelt and soon it was blunt. Only when he used the claws could he at last make a cut.

This hide saved the life of Hercules many times over, as nothing could pierce it, not even the claws or teeth of the Nemean lion.

When Hera sent Hercules into such a maddened rage that he killed his sons, believing they were enemies, he was told that the only way to atone for his sins was to seek out King Eurystheus, and do his bidding without question or complaint. This was the beginning of the twelve labors.

An enormous lion had been ravaging the countryside and Erystheus sent Hercules to deal with it, thinking he would perish in the attempt. All along the way, he passed terrified peasants who offered to sacrifice to Zeus so that he would die an easy death The lion itself was said to have fallen from the moon and its lair was a terrible sight, littered with the carcasses of animals and the corpses of men and women. This time, Hercules had with him an arsenal of weapons, but his arrows and spears just bounced off its back.

With a great roar, the lion sprang at Hercules, and would have ripped him apart with his fell claws, but for the invulnerable hide which he wore. Grappling with the beast, Hercules wrapped a huge arm around its neck and held on for dear life. No matter how the beast tried to shake him off, his deadly grip would not loosen and before long the struggle was over. The Nemean lion was dead and the first labor completed.

NYMPH

According to Homer, the nymphs were the daughters of Zeus. Although not immortal, they occupied a position between men and the gods, leading very long lives. They were often pictured frolicking with the gods, especially pastoral gods like Pan and gods of revelry Dionysus and Bacchus, hunting with Artemis or looking after the flocks in Arcadia with Apollo and Hermes. Sometimes they became involved with men, in rare cases even marrying them. Orpheus, for example, took the nymph Eurydice for his wife.

As spirits of nature they could be wild and unpredictable, and were very dangerous if crossed.

Daphnis, the son of a nymph himself, had his eyes put out for breaking an oath of fidelity to a nymph.

Hylas was lured to his death by the water nymph of a spring where he was drawing water. The legend of Hermaphroditus tells of a beautiful youth who attracted the attentions of Salmacis, another water nymph, who clung to him so fiercely under the water where he was swimming, that their flesh cleaved one to the other and they became one body, uniting both sexes.

As well as water nymphs or naiads, there were oak tree nymphs or dryads, ash tree nymphs, also known as meliads, and sea nymphs, the nerieds. These last were the daughters of Nereus, the Old Man of the Sea, famed for their great beauty, and called on by sailors in peril for their ability to calm the waves and lull the winds to sleep. They were thought to have brought Achilles his armour from Hephaestus, the god of metal working, before the Trojan war.

The Oceanids were the three thousand daughters of Oceanus and Tethys. "Scattered far and wide" according to Hesiod, "haunting everywhere alike the earth and the watery depths", they included Styx and Eurynome, who saved Hephaestus after Hera threw him out of the heavens and gave birth to the Graces when Zeus made love to her.

Other kinds of nymphs were

aseids, nymphs of the grove, and
oreads, or mountain nymphs,
like Echo who lived on Mount
Helicon. One story tells that she
would always distract Hera with
her inane chatter, while the other
nymphs who had been carousing
with Zeus made good their escape.
To punish her, Hera condemned
her to only be able to repeat what
others had said, no matter what
she herself wanted to say.
Another myth tells of her love for
the beautiful youth Narcissus, the
son of the nymph Liriope. He had
room in his heart only for himself
and as she pined, she wasted away
until all that was left was her
voice.

OANNES

Much has been made of the fact that civilization as we know and understand it today is a phenomenon that began about seven thousand years ago and developed incredibly rapidly. In a very short space of time we moved from hunter-gathering to being able to modify our environment, manipulate the genome and send probes millions of miles into outer space. What has made possible such rapid acceleration in human culture and why did mankind advance so little for the previous tens of thousands of years?

One intriguing possibility is that the earth was visited by intelligent extraterrestrial life-forms who shared with mankind the secrets of civilization. Although most talk of UFOs is idle speculation, two pre-eminent astronomers, Dr. I.S. Shklovsky and Dr. Carl Sagan came up with a theory that such alien contact might survive in the form of myths about divine figures, the gods and goddesses of ancient legends.

One story in particular caught their attention, concerning Oannes, a divine being who resembled a merman, that it to say human from the waist up with the tail of a fish.

There is strong evidence to show that the story as it survived in the Babylonian version has its roots in the much older legends of the Sumerians who were the first ever civilization, founded in the valley of the Euphrates and Tigris rivers. Archaeologists are divided as to how long it took for the Sumerian civilization to develop, but it does seem almost instantaneous. According to the legend, Oannes appeared seemingly out of nowhere from the direction of the Persian Gulf.

"This Being, in the day time used to converse with men but took no food at that season, and he gave them insight into letters, and sciences and every kind of art. He taught them to construct houses, to found temples, to compile laws and explained to them the principles of geometrical knowledge. He made them distinguish the seeds of the earth, and showed them how to collect fruits. In short he instructed them in everything which could tend to soften the manners and humanize mankind. From that time, so universal were his instructions, nothing material has been added by way of improvement. When the sun set it was the custom of this Being to plunge again into the sea, and abide all night in the deep for he was amphibious."

OGRE

Ogres are very similar in concept to the Scandinavian troll, which is to say they are also a breed of sub-human oafish brutes that prey on travellers for food, dwelling mostly in caves but sometimes in castles.

Because of their stupidity and cowardice, they present no threat to the brave man who can easily outwit them, but they are a serious danger to women, children and the unwary who can be caught by surprise and overpowered by their great strength.

For weapons they possess nothing more technologically advanced than the club, sometimes spiked, and they often rely on brute force. With enormous bellies, clumsy hands and misshapen bloated faces, their ugliness is legendary. Some ogres are said to be the guardians of treasure and magical articles, like the goose that lays the golden egg in Jack and the Beanstalk. Others live a rude primitive life of squalor and degradation. They all have a penchant for pretty things, often stealing man-made objects or kidnapping princesses, captivated by their beauty.

Many ogres lead a nocturnal existence, and an easy way to defeat them is to leave them stranded above ground when the sun rises, whereupon they are instantly turned to stone.

They feed on carrion and the flesh of their enemies. The color of their skin varies between shades of black, brown and green. They fight with crude weapons of war, quite unable to master the swords-

ORC

Contrary to popular opinion, the word "orc" did not enter the English language through Tolkien. He rather served to revive interest in the word.

In the epic romantic poem "Orlando Furioso" by Ariosto, an orc, described as a savage blind giant with tusks like a boar, traps the king Narandino and his retinue in much the same way that the Cyclops did to Odysseus and his crew. "Orc" also appears in Beowulf to describe the monstrous troll Grendel. "Orcus" was one of the names given to Hades the Lord of the Under-world. "Orca" referred to one of the most feared marine animals, the killer whale and "orco" was the Italian for "ogre".

In Tolkien's "Lord of the Rings", orcs are described as elves captured by the Dark Lord and tortured in his foul pits in Mordor, until they became twisted and deformed abominations, filled with hatred for elves and men, brimming with reckless, destructive energy. They make up the majority of Sauron's army, but cannot travel by day because of the sunlight and are cowardly and prone to squabbling amongst themselves.

manship of men and elves.
Bigger and more brutal than their
close relatives, the goblins, they
have become a staple of role-
playing games like "Dungeons
and Dragons".

PEGASUS

Pegasus was a beautiful white winged horse, who sprang full-formed from the blood of Medusa, when Perseus cut off her head.

While Pegasus was drinking at a stream in Corinth, Athena helped Bellerophon to capture the horse and ride him into battle against the terrible monster, the Chimera. He also helped Bellerophon revenge himself on the wife of the King of Argos, who had tried to have him killed because he would not return her affections.

When Bellerophon tried to fly Pegasus up to the heavens, Zeus sent an enormous gadfly to sting the winged horse and throw the rider. Bellerophon fell to his death and Zeus took Pegasus for his own, making him immortal

and you can still his constellation among the stars at night in autumn if you live in the middle northern hemisphere.

The fountain at Mount Helicon called the Hippocrene was supposed to have first given forth water when one of the hooves of Pegasus struck the earth.

PHAEA

Phaea, meaning the "grey-haired one", was the wild sow of Crommyon and gets its name from the old crone who tended it. It was the daughter of Typhon and Echidna and came to a sticky which they called Phaea, was no insignificant creature, but fierce and hard to master. This sow he [Theseus] went out of his way to encounter and slay, that he might not be thought to perform all his exploits under compulsion, and at the same time because he thought that while a brave man ought to attack villainous men only in self defense, he should seek occasion to risk his life in battle with the nobler beasts. "However, some say that Phaea was a female robber, a woman of murderous

Aegeus, king of Athens was the father of Theseus. But there were rumors that his mother Aethra had been seduced by Poseidon, hence Theseus' almost god-like strength and bravery. After Aethra became pregnant, Aegeus returned to Athens, leaving his sword, shield and sandals under an enormous rock. He told Aethra that when their son was strong enough to move the rock he should come to Athens to claim the kingship as his birthright.

end on the point of Theseus' spear as he journeyed from Troezen to Athens.
Plutarch describes it thus, "Now the Crommyonian sow, and unbridled spirit, who dwelt in Crommyon, called "Sow" because of her wayward life and manners, and was afterwards slain by Theseus."

It was not long before the mighty Theseus was able to recover his father's possessions and he set out for his palace.

Just as Hercules had met two women, Vice and Virtue, who had offered him two different paths through life, there were two ways to Athens, the easy way by sea and the perilous route over land. Needless to say, Theseus chose the latter and he faced six challenges as he passed six

would force passers-by to wash his feet and then kick them off the cliff to a huge man-eating turtle below. He also met some rough justice at the hands of Theseus. The penultimate incarnation of evil was king Cercyon, who challenged travellers to a wrestling contest and then had

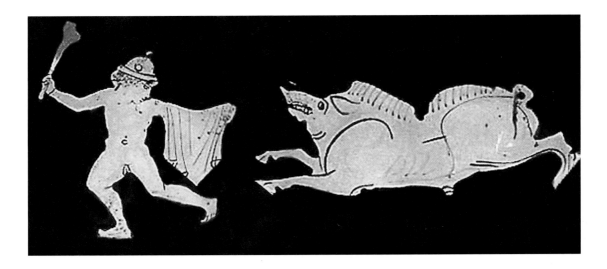

gateways to the Underworld, each guarded by a personification of evil.
At the first Theseus met and vanquished Periphetes, who clubbed his victims into the earth.

At the second stood the bandit Siris, who literally tore his victims limb from limb by tying them between two palm trees bent to the ground, which were then released. Theseus served him a bit of his own cruel medicine and seduced his daughter.

The sow stood at the third entrance and at the fourth Sciron

them killed, but he was no match for our hero.
The last villain was Procrustes who offered weary pilgrims a bed and then either chopped off their feet if they protruded or stretched them on a rack if they were too short. As you no doubt have already guessed he picked on the wrong guy when he encountered Theseus.

phoenix

The phoenix was a large bird, bigger than an eagle, with beautiful golden and scarlet feathers and a hauntingly stirring cry. The descriptions of some authors resemble the bennu, an Egyptian heron, which is often carved on tombs to show the promise of life after death.

Estimates of its life span vary from between 500 and 97,000 years and there is never more than one phoenix alive at any one time. When it realizes that death is near at hand, it builds a nest of spices and sweet-smelling boughs, which is lit by the strong rays of the sun. As the flames lick higher and higher, it sings a mournful song and expires.

From the ashes a new phoenix emerges and flies to Heliopolis, the City of the Sun, with the ashes of its father embalmed in an egg of myrrh to make an offering of them to the Sun God in his sacred temple.

Some sources describe the dying phoenix flying to Heliopolis and sacrificing itself in the Sun God's ceremonial fire.

Scholars generally agree that the connection with the City of the Sun, with fire and rebirth, demonstrate a symbolic representation of the story of the sun, in that there can only ever be one sun in the sky, and although it seems to die each night, travelling through the Underworld to do battle with the forces of darkness and chaos, yet it is miraculously reborn each new morning.

This would have seemed like a promise to the Ancient Egyptians that their own death was but a brief struggle with darkness and fear, after which their souls would rise like the sun to the glorious new dawn of the Afterlife.

This idea appealed to the Christians and shaped their idea of the immortality of the soul and the virgin birth of Christ. The connection of the phoenix to the palm tree - the Greek for palm is "phoinix" and the palm was supposed to live for as long as the phoenix – might also be connected to Palm Sunday and the risen Christ.

A Phoenix attacking an antelope. From a Persian carpet design, 17th or 18th century.

PIXIE

The pixies seem to be a regional variation of the general concept of fairy folk, centered around the west country of England in Devon and Cornwall, much like the brownies in Scotland. Supposedly they were condemned to an existence somewhere between the mortal and the spiritual realms because they were neither good enough to enter Heaven, nor evil enough for Hell. Another explanation posits that they had once been druids with magical powers who refused to recognise Christ and their pagan magic turned in upon itself until they grew smaller and smaller, so small that they almost disappeared altogether.

Seldom seen, more often their mischievous laughter was heard and the effects of their meddling felt, but if you did catch a glimpse the impression was of a little person with sharp ears, wearing green and a tall pointed hat.

Sometimes their presence was betrayed by a sparkling dust in the air or on the ground like pollen in the sunshine.

One of their favorite pranks was to steal horses and ride them all through the night, returning them in the morning too exhausted to work. Another, which could prove fatal, was to confuse travellers crossing the moors, leaving them hopelessly lost.

One way to thwart their magical influence was to always carry a piece of metal, which they found irksome. Another was to remove your coat and turn it inside out, which left them bewildered.

Alternatively you could try to appease them before making your journey by leaving out food and drink, in which case they might even try to help, warding off bad luck and sometimes tidying the house upon your return.

Although belief in pixies has all but faded away, it was once very widespread. As with the fairies it is possible the myths about these little people stem from an encounter of the Celts arriving on the shores of Britain with an elusive tribe of hunter-gatherers.

PYTHON

Python was an enormous she-dragon, the guardian of the oracle at Pytho, later Delphi. In the Homeric Hymn to Apollo, she also raised the monster Typhon who was eventually to challenge Zeus.

Before she was shot dead by Apollo, when he arrived to found his oracle, she preyed on the goats and sheep of the neighboring tribes. The name Python comes from her coils that rotted in the sun by the sacred spring after she died. To honor her, the Pythian games were begun in her memory and the priestesses of the oracle were called Pythia.

Another myth makes Python a male snake, who tried to murder Leto when she was pregnant with Apollo, knowing by his powers of divination that her son would eventually kill him.

Supposedly both versions of the myth symbolise the victory of the celestial spiritual god over the physical forces of the earth.

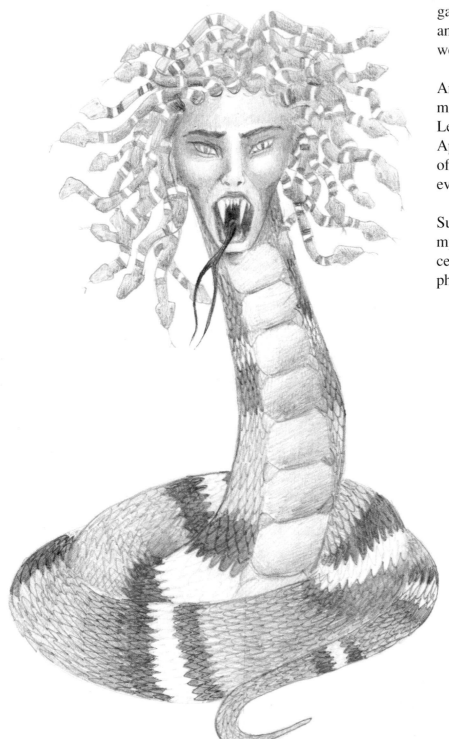

REMORA

The remora is a very real fish that has entered the realm of myth because of its unusual properties. On its back is a dorsal fin with a difference. It has been modified into a "transversely laminated sucking disc" which basically

means that it can attach itself to other fish by forming a vacuum against a flat surface. Any attempt to pull the fish off only serves to make the attachment stronger. If it is pulled forwards, the grip may be broken.

This has led to fishermen using the remora to catch turtles. When a boat sights a turtle, the remora is released with a line tied round its tail and swims straight to the turtle. The attachment is so firm that the turtle can be reeled in and even lifted out of the water.

The remora gets its name from the ancient belief that the fish could even stop a ship from sailing.

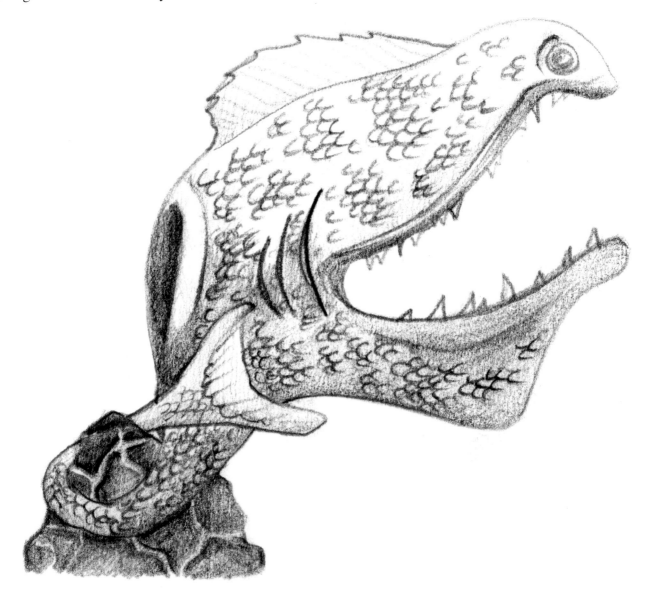

REMORA

CONTINUED

"Remora" means "delay" in Latin and its family name, "echeneis" derives from the Greek "echein", "to hold" and "naus", "ship". Pliny wrote of the fish as causing the defeat of Mark Anthony in the battle of Actium and being responsible for the death of Caligula. In Harry Potter, they are used to anchor boats.

In reality the fish feed off food dropped from the mouths of their hosts, which include manta rays, whales, turtles and sharks. Some are so small that they actually travel inside the mouth.

The appearance of the remora can lead to the mistaken belief that it is travelling upside-down, and this no doubt contributed to its ancient familiar name, Reversus.

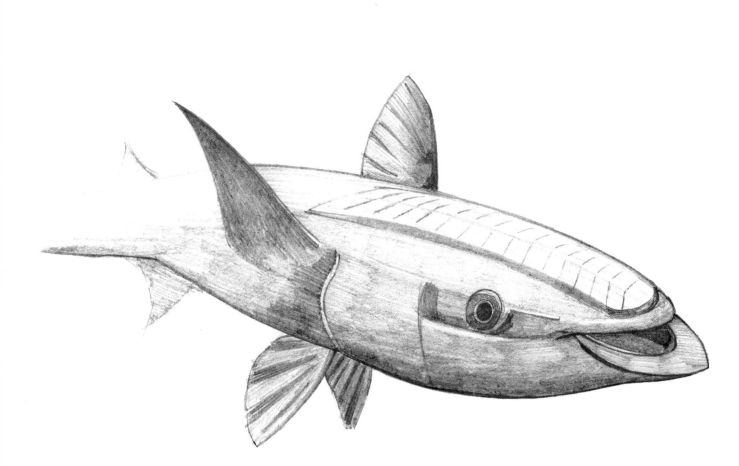

Above: the "real" remora has a sucker pad on top of its head.

ROC

The word roc comes from the Persian "rukh", an enormous bird so large that it was thought to carry off elephants in its talons and drop them into the nest to feed its young.

The roc makes its most famous appearance in literature in the adventures of Sinbad the Sailor.

When he first sees one of the eggs he mistakes it for a vast dome and because he tarries too long, the mother returns from hunting, her presence announced by the sun disappearing from view behind her great wing span. He barely manages to escape with his life and one of his ships is indeed lost as the monstrous bird follows them out to sea with a huge boulder clutched in its talons, which it drops on them.

The origins of this mythological creature may lie with the Aepyornis, the "elephant bird" that lived on Madagascar. Supposedly it was a flightless bird, one of the biggest ever to have existed, with eggs about five times the size of an ostrich egg. Arab traders sailing down the east coast of Africa may have heard stories of this bird or even encountered it if they tried to steal eggs to bring back as souvenirs and gifts. This would have been a terrifying and

ROC
CONTINUED

dangerous experience if the birds were anything like the Australian cassowary, which can disembowel a man with powerful kicks from its claws. With each telling, the details and dimensions of these stories would inevitably become exaggerated.

Another intriguing possibility is that hoaxers may have perpetuated the myth in order to sell fakes to gullible collectors. Marco Polo tells of the Great Kahn of Cathay being presented with a feather of the roc, which was over twelve feet long. Was this evidence of the legendary monster or a dried frond of the sagus ruffia, a palm tree native to the island of Madagascar?

SATYR

According to classical Greek myths, Satyrs were spirits of the woods and fields, symbols of the fertility of Nature. Filled with the exuberance and fecundity of the rising sap, the bursting bud and the swelling fruits, they seemed drunk with life, wild and lascivious. Music, merry-making and lusting after the Maenads and nymphs were their chief preoccupations and wherever the god of wine Dionysus went, they were sure to follow.

Sometimes they were shown with the torso of a man and the legs, ears and tail of a horse, at others with the legs and horns of a goat. Legends tell of one Satyr called Silenus, who was either the foster father or companion of Dionysus. Although an irredeemable old drunkard, at rare moments he could be very wise.

One day, King Midas caught him in his rose garden, by pouring wine into the waters of the spring, where Silenus had gone to quench his thirst. In a melancholy outburst he told Midas that the happiest man was he who was never born at all, the second happiest, he who died the soonest.

In recompense for treating the drunk old Satyr well, Dionysus granted him a wish and foolishly the king asked that whatever he touched would turn to gold. When he realized the consequences, he was told to bathe in the river Pactolus, and ever afterwards the sands on the riverbank glittered in the sun.

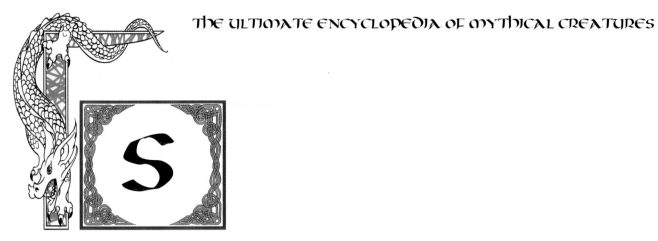

SATYR
CONTINUED

SCYLLA

Scylla was a fearsome monster of Greek legend, who inhabited a cave high up in the straits of Messina. When Ulysses sailed through this narrow channel, he found that he could not avoid passing under her lair, without going perilously near to a whirlpool called the Charybdis. The roar of the waters as they boiled and bubbled, at any moment threatening to suck the ship down to the bottom of the sea, distracted Ulysses and he allowed the ship to drift too close to the other side. Before they knew what was happening, she had thrust her six long necks out of the mouth of the cave and snatched up six sailors. Mercifully the noise of the rushing waters drowned out the screams as they were devoured.

But Scylla had not always been so fearsome. Once, may years before, she had been a beautiful young maiden with whom Glaucus had fallen deeply in love. Glaucus himself had been transformed from a simple fisherman into a mighty sea-god, when he cast his nets from a magical island. Catching sight of Scylla,

SCYLLA CONTINUED

washing on the shore, he declared his love for her, but she took fright and ran away.

He begged the enchantress Circe to cast a spell to woo her heart, but she was a spiteful creature, jealous of Scylla's beauty and instead she bewitched the waters where Scylla bathed, so that her limbs were transformed into writhing snakes and with time Scylla became as ugly and devious on the inside as she was on the outside.

In the end she was turned into a rock jutting out of the sea but she is just as perilous as ever to sailors.

Scylla, as depicted on a 5yh century BC Greek vessel.

SEA SERPENT

One of the most elusive mytho-logical creatures is the gigantic sea serpent. To this day, despite centuries of sightings and tales told in harbor-side inns, despite the extensive surveys of the deepest ocean beds with the latest submarine technology, there does not exist one tangible piece of evidence to prove its existence. Photographs taken of the creature are either hoaxes or too vague to be conclusive. All we have are the writings of rather credulous naturalists based on unverifiable sightings.

The sixteenth century archbishop of Uppsala in Sweden, Olaus Magnus, describes a monster over two hundred feet long and twenty feet around the neck adding, "He hath commonly hair hanging from his neck a cubit long and sharp scales, and is black, and hath flaming shining eyes. This snake disquiets the shippers and he puts his head on high like a pillar and catcheth away men and devours them."

It is important to note that he had not seen this monster himself but was relying on hearsay.
In the eighteenth century we have the recorded eyewitness statement from Hans Egede, a missionary on his way from Norway to Green-land.

"This monster was of so huge a size that coming out of the water, its head reached as high as the mast head, its body was bulky as the ship and three or four times as long. It had a long pointed snout and spouted like a whale-fish, great broad paws and the body seemed covered with shell-work. Its skin was very rugged and uneven. The under part of its body was shaped like an enormous serpent and when it dived again under the water, it plunged backwards into the sea and so raised its tail aloft, which seemed a whole ship's length distant from the bulkiest part of the body."

In his "A Natural History of Norway", the Bishop of Bergen, Erik Pontoppidan, includes the account of a ship's captain who saw and shot a sea snake in August 1746. Unfortunately the creature sank before it could be hooked and hauled overboard.

"The head which it held more than two feet above the surface of the water resembled that of a horse. It was of a greyish color, and the

SEA SERPENT
CONTINUED

mouth was quite black and very large. It had large black eyes and a long white mane, which hung down to the water. Beside the head and neck we saw seven or eight folds or coils of this snake, which were very thick and as far as we could guess there was a fathom's distance between each fold."

The next and possibly most reliable witness statement comes from the Captain of H.M.S. Daedalus, writing after his ship returned to Plymouth from the East Indies.

His report is intriguing because he staked his reputation before the Lords of the Admiralty on its

veracity. His career would have been ruined if he was found to be lying.

"The diameter of the serpent was about fifteen or sixteen inches behind the head, which was without any doubt that of a snake, and it was never during the twenty minutes that it continued in the sight of our glasses, once below the surface of the water. Its color was a dark brown, with yellowish white about the throat. It had no fins, but something like the mane of a horse, or rather a bunch of seaweed, washed about its back."

What was odd about the account was the seeming rigid immobility of the creature and one explanation put forward by L. Sprague de Camp is that the sailors had in fact seen a dugout canoe, abandoned by fishermen after they harpooned a whale shark. The prows of these canoes were often carved and painted to resemble the head and neck of animals.

The whole field of sea serpent investigation fell into disrepute and was never henceforth treated seriously by orthodox scientists after a group of amateurs called the Linnaean Society of

New England mistakenly identified a common black sea snake as the offspring of an enormous sea serpent that was sighted off Gloucester harbour in Massachusetts. It was supposed that the serpent had come inshore to lay its eggs and such was the zeal to prove this theory that scientific rigour was abandoned and the field ever after was tainted with embarrassing credulousness.

Sightings grew few and far between. The next one of note was reported by the U-boat captain Georg Gunther Freiherr von Forstner who claimed that

SEA SERPENT
CONTINUED

after he sank the British steamer Iberion there was a huge underwater explosion which threw up an enormous sea monster, in its last throes, like a sixty foot long crocodile with an elongated neck.

There have however been a few treatises in the twentieth century, the most notable of which were "The Case for the Sea Serpent" in 1930 by Lieutenant Commander Rupert T. Gould and "In the Wake of the Sea Serpents" by Bernard Heuvelmans in 1968.

Interestingly, in the latter, the case is put that nine large hitherto unclassified marine animals are responsible for the sightings-two huge reptiles, an enormous eel, five gigantic sea mammals and something called a Yellow Belly. But since the publication of the book nothing has turned up to support his theory and it is very unlikely that there exist five unknown species of sea mammals, which after all have to come to the surface to breathe.

Without any material evidence such as remains washed up on the shore, time is running out for the sea serpent.

SIREN

In classical art, sirens were depicted in two ways, either as women with birds' legs and wings or as birds with the faces of women. There is also disagreement as to whether their father was the sea god Phorcys or the river god Achelous.

Their singing was so beautiful that it would lure sailors to their death, driving their ships onto jagged rocks in the desperate attempt to draw nearer to the singing.

Depending on whom you read, there were either two sirens who inhabited an island between Aea and the rocks of Scylla or three who lived on the coast of Italy by Napoli.

They are similar in conception and appearance to the harpies, and they may both have a common ancestor in the oriental winged ghosts that would snatch the souls of the living.

Odysseus was able to hear the beautiful music without suffering the fate of so many sailors by plugging the ears of his crew with wax and lashing himself to the mast so he could not take his ship onto the rocks.

When Jason sailed that way with the Argonauts, the bard Orpheus sang so sweetly that the sailors ignored the sirens and like the sphinx they destroyed themselves.

SIREN
CONTINUED

sphinx

There are two famous examples of sphinxes with which we are familiar today. One is the huge monument guarding the pyramids at Giza. The other is the sphinx who figures in the story of Oedipus. They differ in two important respects.

The monument is a male lion with the face of the King Khafre, although some scholars maintain it is the face of Khufu, the builder of the tallest of the three pyramids.
For the Egyptians, the sphinx was a protective symbol combining the power and strength of the lion with the royalty of the pharaoh. This both cowed the populace into submission and reassured them that he could protect them from such forces of chaos as invasion and drought.

Because lions could see in the dark, they were thought to be able to detect ghosts and devils that lurked in the desert, lying in wait for the unwary. Statues of sphinxes often stood guard at the entrance to houses to ward off evil spirits, and on a monumental scale this is the function of the sphinx at Giza.

Some archaeologists think that there was once a second sphinx lying out to the west and as a pair they represented Shu and Tefnut, guarding the eastern and western gates of the horizon, through which the sun god Ra would pass each morning and evening.

The sphinx in the Greek myth however has been transformed over the centuries into a female figure, with wings and breasts. According to some scholars she is the daughter of Chimaera and Orthrus, according to others the daughter of Echidna and Typhon. She is no longer protective, on the contrary she has become a destructive force, ravaging the countryside around Thebes asking her riddle, "What goes

S

who could not solve it. When Oedipus gives the correct answer, "Man...for as an infant he crawls on all fours, in his prime he walks upright and in his dotage he leans on a staff", the Sphinx devours herself. But not before becoming the instrument of the fulfillment of the curse that he should wed his mother, for the king had decreed that whosoever

should kill the sphinx would have the hand of his sister, Jocasta, Oedipus's mother.

To this day, the sphinx is still used in figures of speech to denote wisdom and ineffable mystery.

on four feet in the morning, two in the afternoon and three in the evening?" and devouring all those

SPRING HEELED JACK

Half a century before London became the stalking ground of the notorious serial killer known as Jack the Ripper, another Jack had Londoners trembling behind closed doors as the sun went down and the thick fog closed in. This was Spring-Heeled Jack and he is perhaps the strangest and most enigmatic of the colorful and frightening characters to have haunted the city in all its long history.

In 1838, Jane Alsop of Bearbind Lane in Lambeth told the police that she had answered the door late one evening to a tall figure dressed in a black cloak, who claimed to be a policeman. He asked her to bring out a lantern and when she did so, "he threw off his outer garment, and applying the lighted candle to his breast, presented a most hideous and frightful appearance, and vomited forth a quantity of blue and white flame from his mouth, and his eyes resembled red balls of fire".

He then tried to grab her "catching her part by the dress and the back part of her neck, placed her head under one of his arms, and commenced tearing her gown with his claws, which she was certain were of some metallic substance." One of Jane's sisters came running at the sound of her screams, but upon seeing the figure "was so alarmed at his appearance, that

S

SPRING HEELED JACK
CONTINUED

she was afraid to approach or render any assistance."

A third sister was made of sterner stuff and managed to drag Jane away from his grip, which was so strong that "a quantity of hair was torn away".

When making a statement to the police, Jane described him as wearing "a large helmet, and his dress appeared to resemble white oil skin."

Not long afterwards another woman was attacked, according to the police report, "by a tall thin man, enveloped in a long black cloak."

"In front of him he was carrying what looked like a bull's eye lantern. With one bound he was in front of her, and before she had a chance to move, he belched blue flames from his mouth into her face."

In both these incidents, the strange figure evaded capture by bounding away in a manner that led journalists to conjecture that he might have springs attached to his feet.

In one case he was said to have jumped right over a tall hedge. London was gripped by hysteria, which soon spread to other towns and cities, and as often happens in such cases, descriptions of the creature were wildly distorted until he became the devil himself with horns and cloven feet.

He was spotted climbing a church spire in Limehouse, with eyes aflame, leering at the onlookers in the street below. He was also reported to have thrown a prostitute into the Thames at Jacob's Island in Bermondsey.

Many of these sightings were undoubtedly the work of malicious pranksters, and one youth was apprehended in Warwickshire, wrapped in a sheet with a grotesque mask on his head and springs on his heels.

As no arrest was forthcoming, the fever died down, and Spring-Heeled Jack seemed to have returned, as one journalist put it, "to the fiery depths whence he came" although there were sporadic sightings and one major episode in the 1860s when a mob appeared to have cornered the monster but he sprang away in one of his characteristic bounds.

The author Peter Haining has suggested in his book "The Legend and Bizarre crimes of Spring-Heeled Jack" that the perpetrator was a fire-eater, and his mask and helmet protected his face from the flames. Perhaps he did in fact wear springs on his shoes.

As time wore on Spring-Heeled Jack evolved into a crime-fighting superhero much like the modern day Spiderman, and he featured heavily in the Victorian Penny Dreadfuls, the cheap and illustrated "comic books" of the day, which pandered to the taste for sensationalist lurid tales of sex and violence.

He even appeared on stage in plays performed in the West End theatres such as "Spring-Heeled Jack; or the Felon's Wrong". There was an arrest in 1878 of a "most strong and gymnastically-inclined" young soldier in Aldershot on the charge of impersonating Spring-Heeled Jack, but there was insufficient evidence and the case collapsed.

And so Spring-Heeled Jack, much like his namesake Jack the Ripper, disappeared from history, leaving behind a puzzle that is still unsolved.

SPRITE

The word "sprite" is a catch-all reference to every kind of goblin, elf, fairy, and originally also ghost. Although this last meaning has fallen away with modern usage, it can be seen in the derivation of the word from the Latin "spiritus" or "spirit" and is still evident in the related word "sprightly" meaning "spirited" or "vivacious".

Belief in these creatures, which were associated with the four elements, was very widespread and even influenced men of science such as Paracelsus, the Swiss Physician who had such an influence on medicine during the Renaissance. In a serious academic treatise, he wrote of "the sylphs of the air, the salamanders of fire, the undines or nymphs of water and the gnomes of the earth."

According to him, they lived lives very similar those of men and women but they did not possess a soul. As well as being able to disappear and reappear wherever they so desired, they could influence the course of human destiny, often to the downfall of whoever had offended them.

It was thought that sprites were once angels who had not taken sides when Lucifer challenged the authority of God, waiting to see who would triumph and for this, their punishment was to be banished from Heaven and bound to the material plane. Other beliefs were that they were the ghosts of children who had died before being baptized or the souls of the dead who were neither good enough to enter Heaven nor bad enough to go to Hell.

Much of our modern understanding of sprites comes from fairy tales, as collected and retold by the Brothers Grimm and the French poet Charles Perrault who wrote "Comtes de ma mere l'Oye" in 1697, which we know as "Tales of Mother Goose".

Originally many sprites would have been as big if not taller than humans, of an ethereal and beautiful appearance. But they have degenerated over the years into tiny, often winged creatures, exemplified in the woodland

S

fairies of Shakespeare's "A Midsummer Night's Dream".

Supposedly there were two kinds of sprite. One lived in communities governed by a king and queen with laws and social mores, much like their human neighbors. The other kind was solitary, associated with a particular tree, grove or spring. Their green and gold clothing was spun from gossamer, leaves and vines and they lived in toadstools and buttercups.

squonk

The squonk made its first appearance in the annals of mythological bestiaries in the nineteenth century, supposedly because the logging industry made incursions into its territory in the Hemlock forests of Northern Pennsylvania.

In such books as "Fearsome creatures of the lumberwoods, with a few desert and mountain beasts" written in 1910 by Willliam T. Cox, it is described as being hideously ugly, with loose skin that sags in bags from its belly, and dotted with warts and strange ulcerous growths. For this reason it shuns the presence not just of man but every creature of the woods, and lives a solitary life, feeling sorry for itself, often bursting into uncontrollable fits of tears.

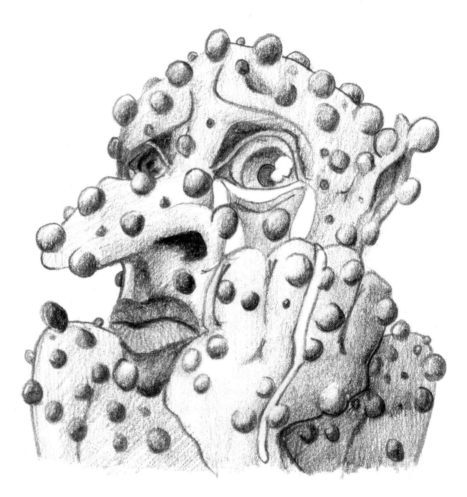

In fact so given to crying and sorrow is the squonk that if captured it will completely dissolve into a fluid, as one hunter found upon examining his sack, which was suddenly very light, with water leaking through the material. That is how it got its Latin name, "Lacrimacorpus dissolvens", which means "the body dissolves into tears".

This melancholic existence has won it a place in the hearts of many artists and musicians who have fondly remembered it in such songs as "Squonk", sung by Phil Collins and "Any major dude will tell you" by Steely Dan. And there is even a Dutch jazz rock band named after the poor little fellow, "The Mighty Squonk".

STYMPHALIAN BIRDS

For his sixth labor, Eurystheus sends Hercules to drive away the Stymphalian birds, which belonged to Ares, the god of war.

This was an awesome task for the birds were protected by brass feathers which fell to the earth like a meteor shower when they molted, their claws and beaks were also brass and they had the nasty habit of flying straight at their targets and running them through. No armor could withstand such an assault. On top of all this they had a penchant for human flesh.

Athena, who favored Hercules, procured from Hephaestus, the god of fire and the smithy, a pair of brass castanets, and when he clashed them together from the top of a mountain, the noise was such that it drove the birds mad and in a frenzy they rushed away, several of them falling to his well-aimed arrows.

TRITON

The original triton was the son of Poseidon and the nereid Amphitrite, but as tales of his exploits spread, he became just one of many tritons who accompanied Poseidon.

They liked nothing better than to play in the waves with the nereids, although they could become bothersome, in one case attacking the women of Tanagra when they came to the shore to purify themselves before making offerings to Dionysus. In answer to their prayers, Dionysus intervened and chased them off.

In another instance a triton that had been menacing fishing boats was lured onto the beach with a bowl of wine. Intoxicated, he collapsed and one of the townspeople chopped off his head.

According to Pausanias, who claims to have seen this specimen, the head was covered with hair like a marsh frog, the eyes were blue, the nose human but the teeth sharp. The fingers resembled a man's but the skin was covered in scales, with gills like a fish and a dolphin's tail.

TROLL

In Scandinavian folklore, trolls are a breed of powerful, ugly monsters that walk upright, with strong grasping arms and stout stumpy legs. They can either be hairless or covered with thick matted dirty hair. Their skin ranges from green to blue to black and is covered in warts and calluses.
Peculiarly both "giant" and "dwarf" seem to be interchangeable with "troll".

They are usually presented as vicious and bloodthirsty, feasting on human flesh, the scourge of isolated settlements and lone travellers but in some children's tales they are viewed more sympathetically and their reputation is said to be founded on human failings like stupidity, greed and pride. In certain instances they even redeem themselves by helping the hero to overcome some seemingly insurmountable obstacle.

They are said to live in places shielded from sunlight (which they cannot bear for it hurts their eyes and burns their skin) such as underneath bridges, as in the tale of the "Three Billy Goats" or deep within the forest or in caves beneath the mountains. Often a large boulder, which none but the

strongest of men can move, blocks the entrance to their lair.
If wounded in battle but not killed their injuries will completely heal over if they are then allowed to return to their lairs and rest, for their skin has regenerative properties similar to plant tissue.

Like pixies and fairies trolls will often steal a human child and replace it with one of their own, so it can benefit from breast milk. They are also fascinated with beauty and their lairs are a treasure-trove of pretty things, stolen from humans. They sit dumbfounded in the dark, staring endlessly at these valuables,

absolutely incapable of replicating such craftsmanship.

For the same reason they will kidnap beautiful girls and although not in danger of physical violence, for all the troll wants to do is stare at them, they are in danger of wasting away as the troll's needs are completely alien to that of a human.

In some tales trolls are said to hate noise, especially church bells and the word for boulders lying near churches is "jattescast" which means "giant thrown", indicating the level of violence to which

the noise drives them. This stems from a time when Thor used to throw his hammer at them and as human settlements encroach into their territory the sounds of human labour, especially that of the smithy, drives them further and further into the wildest and most inaccessible places.

This chimes in with an interesting theory that the concept of the troll is a distant recollection of a time when our Cro-magnon ancestors moved into Europe and encountered the last remaining Neanderthals before they died out.

TYPHON

In the Homeric hymn to Apollo, Hera gave birth to Typhon without a father to show Zeus, who had given birth to Athena without a mother, that she could do it too. She had already produced one offspring in this way, Hephaestus, but he was lame and she had rejected him.

Gaia answered Hera's prayers for a son even stronger than Zeus, and the progeny was a truly hideous monster, whom Hera could not raise by herself, so she gave him to the snake Python.

Around his neck hundreds of snakes hissed, with eyes aflame. When they opened their mouths abominable sounds came out over their black tongues-roaring, barking, growling, the clashing of cymbals and the banging of great drums. He belched fire and smoke from his lips and instead of fingers and legs he had writhing venomous snakes. So huge was he, that his head reached the stars and when he spread out his arms he encompassed both the eastern and western horizons.

When he met Zeus in battle, the earth shook as though it might split asunder.

"A conflagration gripped the purple sea, from the god's thunder and lightning and the monster's fire, from the flaming bolt and the tornado winds..."

The gods of Mount Olympus were so frightened that they fled to Egypt and disguised themselves as animals. But in the end Typhon could not withstand the thunderbolts of Zeus and he was thrown into the sulphurous pits of

Tartarus, whence his foul breath still causes misery to sailors in the form of typhoons.

In another version, Typhon got close in to grapple with Zeus, where he could not use his thunderbolts. Zeus drew his sickle to strike at him, but Typhon's strength was such that he was able to seize it. Slicing through the sinews of his hands and feet, he

carried Zeus back to his cave and gave the sinews to the she-dragon Delphyne to guard. But Hermes and Aegipan were too guileful for the dumb brute and stole them back.

Once reunited with his sinews, Zeus's wrath was terrible and his thunderbolts rained down on Typhon. The Fates cheated him by feeding him fruits that sapped his

strength and finally Zeus hurled Mount Etna on top of him and its weight pressed Typhon to the ground.

Trapped forever, occasionally he tries to lift the mountain and his fiery breath pours forth with the effort.

UNICORN

Picture a unicorn and you immediately conjure up the classic tall white horse, gentle and graceful, with its kind eyes and flowing white mane and of course the single needle-sharp horn.

But the original creature was strikingly different, about the size of a goat, with a lion's tail, cloven hooves, and that unique horn. The Greek historian, Ctesia, writing in about 400 BC, tells of a creature with the body of an ass, the feet of a goat, a purple head that resembled a deer's, and a horn that was red at the tip, black in the middle and white at the bottom. It is thought he was prompted by information relayed from explorers who had travelled to India.

The origins of this myth are difficult to pin down. It could have

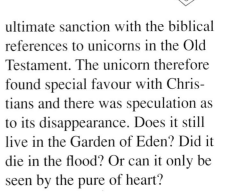

arisen from travellers' tales of the rhinoceros, which have gradually been embellished and distorted.

Marco Polo tells of an animal with the body of an elephant and a pig's head with a horn growing from its brow. But the myth pre-dates Marco Polo by a long time. If you ever catch sight of an oryx from the side, note how the horn on the far side is perfectly covered by the one in front to give the impression of a single horn. Could this have given rise to the legend?

The tusk of the narwhal, which grows up to ten feet long, could be behind it all. Viking traders took these horns to ports all over Europe and further afield, jealous-ly guarding the location of their breeding grounds, and perhaps spinning tall tales to push up the prices. As these stories spread the horns became famed for all kinds of wondrous properties, such as purifying dirty water, defeat-ing poison and even proving the virginity of a prospective match! Perhaps this is why it came to be thought that only a virgin could tame a unicorn and indeed a popular trick in folklore was to lull a unicorn to sleep on the lap of a virgin and then catch him in a net.

Royal families were not immune to the claims of the narwhal tusk traders and Queen Elizabeth 1 paid 10,000 pounds for one which would have bought her another castle to add to her collection! The Danish throne is also adorned with them and two crossed tusks frame the entrance to the imperial palace in Japan.

One reason why so many people may have believed in the existence of the unicorn, is that many monks wrote works of natural history in which they included such fabulous beasts and as men of God their word was taken as truth. A book written by Sir John Mandeville called "The Traveller's Tales" in which he claimed to have seen a unicorn, sparked off a whole series of sightings, much as was the case with the Loch Ness monster in this century.

And of course there was the

ultimate sanction with the biblical references to unicorns in the Old Testament. The unicorn therefore found special favour with Chris-tians and there was speculation as to its disappearance. Does it still live in the Garden of Eden? Did it die in the flood? Or can it only be seen by the pure of heart?

Its association with virginity and purity led to its depiction in religious paintings often symbol-izing Christ himself, as in the paintings of the Virgin Mary with a unicorn in her lap.

It also appeared on the coats-of-

UNICORN
CONTINUED

arms of many English noblemen along with the rose to signify constancy and strength.

The unicorn however is a universal myth. There is a Chinese version called Ki-Lin whose appearance was supposed to presage the birth of wise men and great leaders. This myth, possibly the first ever appearance of the unicorn, stretches back almost to the beginning of the third millennium BC.

He was a very impressive creature, more like a dragon than a horse, with a backward facing horn. In his voice was the music of the heavenly spheres and although he was lord of all the animals, he was so noble and gentle that he took great care not to step on them, lifting his hooves high in the air as he walked. Not only was he beautiful, he was also wise, with the accumulated wisdom he gained living to a thousand years and not even the most cunning of men could catch him.

VAMPIRE

The legend of the vampire has its roots in the folklore of the regions around the Carpathian and Transylvanian mountains in Central Europe. Up until as recently as the early twentieth century, the pace of change in these isolated parts was very slow, and they were untouched, not only by the industrialization of much of the rest of Europe, but also by the new rational schools of thought which rejected the old superstitious ways.

Belief in the Evil Eye, the power of charms and curses, and blood-sucking vampires were commonplace and Christianity could do little to displace them.

Our modern-day acquaintance with the vampire cult stems from the book written by Bram Stoker in 1897. If you haven't actually read it, any vampire film you may have seen is bound to have borrowed heavily from it.

The myth first turns up in Western European literature in the late eighteenth century in Goethe's "Braut von Korinth", although tales had been filtering through to civilization for a long time, brought back by intrepid travellers and traders.

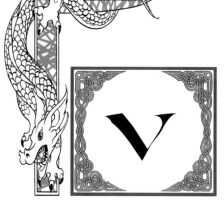

One written account, purporting to be the statement of an eyewitness present at the destruction of a vampire, who had been plaguing a nearby village, describes how, "It leaned to one side, the skin was fresh and ruddy, the nails grown long and evilly crooked, the mouth slobbered with blood from its last night's repast. Accordingly a stake was driven through the chest of the vampire, who uttered a terrible screech whilst blood poured in quantities from the wound. Then it was burned with ashes."

Stories of the blood-sucking vampire appealed to the sensation-seeking mind of Lord Byron and he incorporated them into his poem The Giaour :

"But first, on earth as Vampire sent,
Thy corse shall from its tomb be rent:
Then ghastly haunt thy native place,
And suck the blood of all thy race;
Then from thy daughter, sister, wife,
At midnight drain the stream of life."

When Lord Byron and his friends, Mr. and Mrs. Shelley, Dr. Polidori and M.G.Lewis stayed together in a house by Lake Geneva,

bad weather forced them to stay indoors. They decided each to write a story. Mary Shelley came up with an idea that would become "Frankenstein", and Byron composed part of a tale of terror which Dr. Polidori later turned into "The Vampire", the first full-length vampire novel of its kind. It spawned the serial publication of "V arney, the Vampire" in 1847, which in turn inspired Bram Stoker's "Dracula".

And indeed there is something

of the Byronic hero about Count Dracula. He is the epitome of the "mad, bad and dangerous-to-know" scoundrel, who is literally irresistible to women, once they have experienced his love bite. The dark and forbidding castle,

the woman in peril, the obsession with death and resurrection, are all classic ingredients of the Gothic novels which were so popular at the end of the seventeenth century and reached their apotheosis in the stories of Edgar Allen Poe.

Bram Stoker's Dracula is a descendent of Vlad the Impaler, a fifteenth century Transylvanian ruler who was so named because of his penchant for impaling his enemies on great stakes. One chronicle tells that after one battle the countryside was swathed, for as far as the eye could see, in a forest of these stakes and the air was full of the groans of dying men. Indeed such was his cruelty, that when one of his own retinue had the temerity to complain

about the stench of all the corpses, Vlad cut off his nose.

Another famous "vampire", who probably inspired Stoker was countess Elisabeth Bathory of Hungary who was said to have kept young peasant maidens locked up in her castle so that she could bathe in their blood. This, she believed, would give her eternal youth.
The vampire legend would not be so pervasive in the collective consciousness if it was just an off-shoot of the blood-sucking demons that haunt the folklore of almost all cultures around the world. It has become inextricably linked with the fear of contamination that has arisen wherever people live in close proximity to one another.

The memory of the Black Death and the possibility of its return has haunted the collective dream of Western society ever since it died away. It is no coincidence that Dracula arrives on the shores of England by ship, as the Bubonic Plague was supposed to have done, and his plan is to make London his stalking ground, where his infectious bite will spread terror and mayhem as quickly as possible.

WEREWOLF

The werewolf, after the vampire, must be the most well-known mythical monster of all and it is not just Hollywood and Hammer Horrors who have made him famous. Myths of werewolves have been around since the dawn of time.

The word "lycanthropy", a medical condition which describes a belief that one is possessed by the spirit of a wolf, comes from "lykos" meaning "wolf" and "anthropos" meaning "man", and in turn derives from the myth of King Lycaon of Arcadia in ancient Greece.

There are several different versions of the legend. Either he tempted Zeus, who had come to his court disguised as a traveller, with the flesh of a child he had slain, or he wanted to bribe Zeus with the offer, or he was too mean to slay an ox to feed his distinguished guest and tried to pass off a dish of human meat in its place. According to another version it was his son whom he offered. Zeus was so disgusted and so angered with this foul deed that he turned Lycaon into a wolf, that his true beastly nature might be plain for all to see.

Thereafter, at an annual sacrifice on the same spot, known as Mount Lycaeus, a man was said to turn into a wolf and could not turn back unless he abstained from human flesh for ten years.

This is probably the origin of the myth in Europe but there are similar beliefs in stories of men metamorphosing into wild animals in remote areas across the globe. The only real difference is that in place of a wolf they feature the locally most feared predator. In India they might feature the tiger, in Africa the hyena, leopard or lion, in South America the jaguar.

From Norse history we have the phenomenon of the "berserker", which comes from the Norse for "ber" meaning "bear" and "serk", meaning "skin". These fearsome warriors were renowned for their ferocious behavior on the battlefield. Although the heat of battle

198

brought out the bestial instincts within all men, these berserkers went one step further, transported into a bloody rage that knew no bounds, killing anything in their path, even men on their own side. In mediaeval France, it was more common to be accused of being a werewolf than a witch and in the sixteenth century there were over 30,000 such trials.

One possible reason for the preva-lence of such cases was the lack of understanding of the phenome-non of the serial killer, who might kill to satisfy an insane blood lust. According to contemporary thinking, such homicidal impulses could not be traced to aberrations within the brain. Rather they had their source in external influences, particularly the desire of the Devil to thwart God's offer of salvation through Christ to mankind.

Before the advent of modern criminal investigative methods it would have been quite easy for a serial killer to kill with impunity and with a transient population and no effective communication between borders, people might often disappear and never be missed.

If someone stumbled across the abhorrent aftermath of such a frenzied killing they might well

W

WEREWOLF
CONTINUED

have difficulty believing that this was the work of a man.

There were several different ways in which a man could become a werewolf.

Men and indeed women were not always turned into werewolves against their will by the bite of another werewolf. Sometimes they actively sought to transform themselves.

According to much German folklore, a strap or belt was needed. This could be made from the hide and fur of a wolf, or a strip of skin from the back of a hanged man. Sometimes the Devil gave this strap as a token and once accepted it could never be renounced.

Another way was to stand within a circle in a graveyard on a full moon and rub a specially prepared ointment into the skin while reciting magical verses. This ointment contained amongst other ingredients Belladonna and nightshade and henbane dissolved in pig fat and alcohol and supposedly fur began to sprout from the skin as the devilish incantations were repeated.

Many stories, such as those

gathered by the brothers Grimm, follow a similar pattern and are clearly related.

For example there is the recurring case of the poor old woman, who always has fresh meat on her table. One night an envious neighbor follows her to the sheep pen and watches aghast as she attacks and kills one of the livestock.

Then there are the three woodcutters who take a nap while waiting

for their lunch to arrive from the village. One of them does not trust the other and he pretends to fall asleep, with one eye open. He watches in horror as this man is transformed into a ravening beast and devours a whole horse. Later, on their return to the village, he complains of a stomach ache.

"That is no surprise!" he is told. "Considering what you have just eaten!"

"If you had told me earlier what you had seen" is the dark reply, "you would not have left the forest..."

The other common motif is the discovery of the identity of the werewolf by managing to wound the werewolf and then finding a similarly injured man or woman. It is not improbable that stories of werewolves might have arisen by such coincidences occurring entirely innocently, especially when men were working alone with farm tools, such as axes and scythes, unable to prove that they had injured themselves. Accusations of "werewolfery" may also have been entirely unfounded and malicious, as was often the case in witchcraft trials. Envy of a neighbor's material possessions could have played a big part.

But the link to mental illness is strongest. This does not just mean that they were misdiagnosing various forms of dementia. Even today there are many people who wholeheartedly believe that when the moon is full they become transformed into a wolf.

As for coming face to face with a werewolf, in the middle ages it was thought that if you threw a piece of metal over his head or called out his name, then he would turn back into human form.

Nowadays, you have to be better prepared, with a gun and a silver bullet in your pocket. And just in case you think this is a mere fanciful notion, bear in mind the story of the Morbach Monster. Morbach in Germany is near Wittlington, where, according to legend, the last werewolf was killed. There is a candle on a shrine to mark the exact spot and should the candle ever die, the werewolf will return.

One night, as recently as 1988, Airforce Base security guards on patrol saw that the candle had been extinguished, and just then they heard the wail of the perimeter alarm echoing ominously in the night.

A little later, one of the guards saw a large wolf-like animal rear up onto its hind legs and then leap over the fence which stood over eight feet high. His Alsatian was so terrified that it was unable to go on working and had to be retired!

YALE

It is possible that the word "yale" comes from the Hebrew for mountain goat, "yael".

We first encounter it in Pliny's Natural History. Supposedly it resembled a cross between an antelope and a goat. It had tusks and thick backwards-curving horns that it could turn towards the front to face its attacker. Other accounts describe a beast with the tail of an elephant and the jaws of a boar, which fought with one horn turned back so that it could be swivelled forwards if the front one was damaged.

It hailed from the then exotic land of Ethiopia and was the mortal enemy of the basilisk, which would try to sting it in the eyes and make them swell until they burst.

Its staunch defiance when under attack made it a popular choice as a supporter in the heraldry of noble families, that is to say one of the creatures that stand either side of, or hold up, the coat-of-arms.

To this day you can still see them over the entrance of Christ College and St. John's in Cambridge.

ZOMBIE

A zombie is essentially a reanimated corpse. According to the superstitions of the West African religions brought over to the Caribbean on the slave ships, a witch-doctor could raise a dead man from his grave and enslave him to his will. Of course not all witch-doctors worked such black and sinister magic, most were healers, but there were rumored to be very malevolent and powerful practitioners of the dark arts who sought to increase their wealth by having an army of servants who would do their bidding without question, needing neither food nor rest.

Voodoo, which is practised in Haiti, is the most commonly known of these religions, although Obeah in Jamaica, Santeria in Cuba, and Orisha in Brazil are very similar.

The prospect of becoming a zombie was particularly abhorrent to slaves, who had spent their lives in the service of another and wished for eternal rest after passing away, not ceaseless toil. The measures they took to protect the bodies of their loved ones were similar in many ways to those taken by British citizens in the nineteenth century when

grave robbers and body-snatchers haunted the cemeteries waiting for fresh corpses to dig up and sell to anatomists for dissection.

Many islanders who prospered legitimately were jealously accused of owning zombies. Bakers, and other tradesmen who worked at night, were especially prone to suspicion.

Documented cases are extremely rare and of course hard to prove, based as they are on hearsay evidence.

In 1938, a girl, supposed to have died three years earlier, was spotted by friends working for a man of questionable virtue. She was so unreceptive to attempts to engage her in conversation as to be virtually mute and her movements were strange and unnatural, as though she were sleepwalking.

If the story is to be believed, the grave where she was reputedly buried was opened and found to be empty. This sparked off rumors that a local witch-doctor was supposed to have owned a female zombie, rumors that were

cannot speak up for themselves. Others stem from malicious gossip. It is possible that the belief has its origins in cases of wrongful pronouncement of death, and subsequent escape from the grave. If a person were deprived of oxygen for long enough, the brain damage would result in a "zombified" state. Such attempts to break out of a coffin may have given rise to the European belief in vampires.

Funnily enough, the European belief in a hypnotist's power over the mind of his subject, is comparable to the relationship of the witch-doctor to the zombie. Movies such as "Dr. Caligari's Cabinet" and "Svengali" explore this theme.

And it might just be possible, with a certain amount of fascination on the part of a witch-doctor, combined with the skilled use of drugs and the conviction of the victim, to create a zombie from a living person, although this condition would be temporary.

Scientific attempts to prove or disprove the myth have tended to make one sceptical of the claims of the witch-doctor. The author Francis Huxley conducted his own researches and uncovered several fraudulent attempts to deceive incredulous persons by "unearthing" a zombie. Apparently a man had been buried and fed oxygen through a hose.

The recent use of DNA testing to examine a claim that a man had found his dead brother living as a zombie proved that the two men could not be related.

later confirmed by the wife of the witch-doctor who had since died. It is more than probable that in so doing, the woman, almost certainly a voodoo priestess herself, was trying to impress her enemies or rivals with her husband's, and by extension her own, power. The outcome of the story is that the girl was taken by a Catholic Priest to a convent in France, but never recovered sufficiently to tell her side of the story.

Another account tells of a girl who wandered into the fields one day where farmhands were working and several of them, one among them a relative, recognized her, even though she supposedly died several years before. This time the rumor was that her husband had poisoned her and paid a witch-doctor to resurrect her as his slave.

Many of these cases undoubtedly involve the mentally ill, who can seem to be in a trance-like state with no will of their own and

INDEX